MW00636109

6/17/13

Marion -

Happy #
70 !

Best wishes,

McClernd

STONE SOUP COTTAGE

Stone Soup Cottage
A Vignette of Seasonal Recipes

Carl and Nancy McConnell
Photographs by Carmen Troesser

Copyright © 2011 by Carl and Nancy McConnell
Photographs © 2011 by Carmen Troesser

Designed by Amy Kaller

ISBN: 978-0-615-47380-2

Printed in the U.S.A.

Stone Soup Cottage is a trademark of Stone Soup Holdings, LLC.

All rights reserved. No part of this book may be reproduced in any form or by any electronic or mechanical means, including information storage or retrieval systems, without permission in writing from the publisher, except by a reviewer, who may quote brief passages in review.

Orders: (636) 244-2233
www.stonesoupcottage.com
info@stonesoupcottage.com

GIVING THANKS

First, to God, who makes everything possible. Thank you for feeding our souls, the only nourishment we need.

To our family, for their unconditional support in this crazy dream. Thank you for letting us fly and not ever asking to where we are flying.

To our precious boys, Christian and Colin, thank you for making us better people every day. We would be nothing but lost without you.

To Noel, thank you for trusting in us and never asking why, what for or "really", as well as graciously taking care of our guests night after night…you are the soul of the Cottage and we are grateful for your dedication. You are irreplaceable.

To Carmen, thank you for capturing our dream through your camera lens. Your gentle soul and deep passion for your craft is so beautiful to watch. We are honored to have you photograph our first book.

To the Wiese Family, thank you for letting us play in your "garden." With each season, we are giddy to see what you will grow next. We cherish our friendship.

To Amy, for never once making us feel a project could never be completed. As deadlines came and passed you always made us feel we were right on schedule. Quite brilliant you are and we are eternally grateful.

To Steve, for offering of yourself in your time and talent and supporting the philanthropic aspect of this project. Your gift of storytelling creates memories that last a lifetime.

Finally to Dianne, for introducing us to the Boys and Girls Clubs of St. Charles County and for believing in us and this project. Your generous and unselfish support to so many people is an inspiration. We are honored to have you in our lives both personally and professionally.

With love and gratitude,
Carl and Nancy

A SPECIAL THANK YOU

Thank you to anyone who has helped a child in need whether inspirationally, financially or in mentorship.

The Boys and Girls Clubs of St. Charles County have been part of the St. Charles community since 1955. Currently, more than two thousand young people are being served in the two St. Charles County facilities. The Clubs promote diversity through respect for others and inclusiveness among people.

Nationwide, the Boys and Girls Clubs of America, a network of 3,900 clubs, annually serve 4.6 million children.

Stone Soup Cottage is named after the classic children's fable, "Stone Soup" which outlines the lesson of cooperation and sharing, especially in times of hardship and scarcity. When everyone pitches in and contributes just one thing, the impossible CAN happen. Whether time or talent, the volunteers at the Boys and Girls Clubs of St. Charles County highlight these principles every day in shaping the young lives of children in our community.

We are honored to be touched by such a wonderful organization. A portion of the proceeds of each cook book will be donated to the Boys and Girls Clubs of St. Charles County; little by little, one bit at a time, a child's life can be changed.

For more information about the Boys and Girls Clubs of St. Charles County, please visit their website, www.bgc-stc.org.

Artwork at left by Troy Palmer, age 13. Painted at the Club in 2010, depicting his interpretation of "Stone Soup" after reading the book in an after school art program.

Farm to Fork. Farmer to Chef. Friend to Friend.

So much of what makes Stone Soup Cottage such a special place to dine are the local farmers, foragers and purveyors who share their items with us week after week, season to season. Whether it be delicate squash blossoms plucked that morning before the dew has set in or heady tree mushrooms proudly presented for a nightly risotto, one thing is certain: it takes a dedicated team.

Our partnership with Norman, Ruthanne and daughter Sarah of Wiese Nursery is a prime example. What started out as a tomato here or a squash blossom there grew into a successful business partnership and, most importantly, a life-long friendship.

Partnering with a farm just seconds away from the restaurant allows the freedom many chefs only dream about. Walking through the fields at early morning and harvesting the yield just hours before the guests arrive to dine is a luxury that is never taken for granted.

Wiese Produce began as a small business in 1978. Joe and Frieda Wiese harvested and sold vegetables out of their garage in Cottleville, Missouri, but soon the word got out, and they acquired a large number of local, regular customers. Wiese Produce became a staple, the place you came to when you wanted that perfectly ripe tomato or the sweetest stalk of corn.

Over the years, Joe and Frieda passed along their passion to their son Norman and his family. When Joe passed away, the family decided to continue this tradition. Wiese Nursery and Produce continues to be the heartbeat in the community for the freshest produce. Stone Soup Cottage is honored to showcase their harvest night after night.

pictured on left: Norman and Ruthanne Wiese with grandchildren Ella and Emma, age 2, in their greenhouse.

TABLE OF CONTENTS

Planning the Perfect Menu: From Our Cottage to Yours

So often we are asked how we develop our menus. Since menus at the Cottage change every two to three weeks and and are rarely repeated, it takes quite a bit of research to anticipate what will be coming in from the local farm or fish monger. The menus outlined in the book can certainly be mixed and matched depending on the time of year you are entertaining.

One main rule of thumb is to be conscious of sauces and finishing ingredients if you mix courses within a season. For example, if you start with a heavier, cream based soup, try to have your next course be on the lighter side so as not to overwhelm your guests, especially when cooking in the warmer months. The beauty of this book is to take the guess work out of putting a menu together.

The ingredients utilized in this book are all easy to find, and we have added a source guide at the end of the book for trickier to locate ingredients such as truffles, game birds and finishing oils.

We are so fortunate to have many farmer's markets and independent grocery stores in the area who do an amazing job at providing a wide array of produce, meats, fresh herbs and oils. When you cook with fresh, seasonal and local products, you will save time and money as everything is readily available.

Wine pairings have also been carefully selected to enhance several of the courses in each menu. We ideally pair two whites and two reds at the Cottage, so the menus in this book follow this same principle. The wines are specifically chosen to compliment the flavor profile of each of the main ingredients, sauces or seasonal accents. For ease of reference, the wines are listed first by vintage year followed by name of the producer and region.

The wines presented in each section are specific and are some of our personal favorites at the Cottage, but as long as you stay within the same varietal flavor profiles, you will stay on track. Any reputable local wine purveyor will be able to suggest a good substitution for each wine to fit your own palate and budget.

Most importantly, have fun with the menus. Make them your own and never be too afraid to try something new!

WINTER

6 Course Chef's Winter Tasting Menu

First Course
Garbure Served with Crusty French Bread
Wine Pairing: 2008 Château Lamothe de Haux, Bordeaux France

Second Course
Fresh Fennel and Clementine Salad

Third Course
Sea Bass Wellington with Champagne Sabayon
Wine Pairing: 2007 Kistler Chardonnay Les Noisetiers, Sonoma

Fourth Course
Wild Mushroom Frittata with Velouté

Fifth Course
Game Hen with Quince Butter
Wine Pairing: 2008 Wildekrans Cabernet Franc, South Africa

Sixth Course
Butterscotch Crème
Wine Pairing: NV Niepoort Tawny Port 20 Year Old, Portugal

GARBURE SERVED WITH CRUSTY FRENCH BREAD

[serves 4]

1 quart Cottage chicken stock *(page 167)*
1 pint water
4 ounces salt pork or country ham
2 chicken thighs, skinless
½ yellow onion, diced medium
1 carrot, peeled and rough cut
¼ head cabbage, julienned
½ cup lima beans, fresh
1 turnip, peeled and diced medium

2 cloves of garlic, crushed and minced
4 sprigs fresh thyme leaves, chopped fine
1 bay leaf
4 ounces fennel sausage
dash of crushed red pepper
salt and pepper as needed
drizzle of olive oil, extra virgin
chardonnay as needed

Start by boiling the chicken thighs in salted water for ten minutes. Strain and set aside.

Drizzle the olive oil in a soup pot. Add the salt pork and render until crispy. Remove the crispy salt pork reserving the oil in the pot. Set the pork aside for later use.

Return the pot to medium heat. Add the garlic and crushed red pepper. Sauté the garlic until it is pale brown in color. Add the chicken stock, water, chicken, carrots and onions. Bring to a slow simmer. Add the fennel sausage and bay leaf. Cover and continue to simmer slowly for 45 minutes. Next, add the cabbage, turnips, lima beans and fresh thyme. Cover again and continue cooking for an additional 30 minutes.

Serve the garbure with a splash of chardonnay and warm, crusty French bread.

FRESH FENNEL AND CLEMENTINE SALAD

[serves 4]

FOR THE SALAD
1 small fennel bulb, peeled and sliced paper thin
2 clementine oranges, segmented
a handful of arugula leaves
salt and pepper to taste
drizzle of honey

FOR THE VINAIGRETTE
1 tbsp. shallot, minced
2 tbsp. white vinegar
1 tbsp. water
3 tbsp. orange juice concentrate
1 tbsp. mayonnaise
salt and pepper to taste

FOR THE VINAIGRETTE
Combine all ingredients and mix well.

FOR THE SALAD
Dress fennel and oranges with vinaigrette. Drizzle the arugula greens with honey. Sprinkle with salt and cracked pepper. Serve with fennel and oranges.

Sea Bass Wellington with Champagne Sabayon

[serves 4]

For Sea Bass
4 sea bass fillets, 4 ounce cut
2 tbsp. pistachios, crushed
1 scallion, slivered fine
1 tbsp. mayonnaise
1 tsp. bread crumbs, fine
1 squeeze fresh lemon juice
1 puff pastry sheet, 8.5 ounce
1 egg, whisked
sea salt and ground pepper as needed

For Sabayon
3 egg yolks
3 tbsp. champagne
1 tbsp. fresh lemon juice
3 tbsp. clarified butter
sea salt and cracked white pepper as needed

In a bowl, combine the pistachios, scallions, mayonnaise, lemon juice and bread crumbs. Mix well and set aside.

Dust a flat and clean surface with a quarter cup of flour. Use a rolling pin to roll out the puff pastry sheet to two times the size. Cut into four equal squares. Place a fillet at the bottom of each puff pastry square. Season the fish with salt and pepper. Top the fish with a pistachio mixture. Fold the top of the puff pastry square down and over the fish. Seal the edges with your fingers and place on a non-stick baking sheet. Brush the Wellingtons with the whisked egg. Sprinkle a touch of sea salt over each Wellington and place into a 400 degree oven for ten to fifteen minutes or until golden brown and puffed. Serve immediately with champagne sabayon.

For Sabayon
Prepare a hot water bath using a sauce pot. In a stainless steel bowl, whisk a bit of hot water with egg yolks. Place bowl on top of sauce pot. Vigorously whisk. The yolks will lighten in color and thicken. Drizzle in the clarified butter. Still whisking vigorously, add the champagne and lemon juice.

Continue stirring until the sabayon easily coats and clings to spoon. Adjust the seasoning and serve immediately.

Wild Mushroom Frittata with Velouté

[serves 4]

For Frittata
5 eggs, cracked and whisked
¼ cup milk, whole
½ yellow onion, diced fine
1 cup oyster mushrooms, stemmed and chopped
2 cloves fresh garlic, slivered
drizzle of olive oil, extra virgin
1 ounce clarified butter
dusting of bread crumbs
salt and pepper as needed
parmesan cheese, grated as desired

For Velouté Sauce
2 cups Cottage chicken stock *(page 167)*
2 ounces flour, all-purpose
1 ounce clarified butter
salt and cracked white pepper as needed

For Frittata
Heat the olive oil in a sauté pan. Add garlic and onions. Sauté until tender and add mushrooms. Toss well and continue to sauté until oyster mushrooms have wilted. Season with salt and pepper. Set aside to cool.

Whisk together milk and eggs. Delicately season with salt and pepper. Cover and refrigerate.

Prepare four 6 ounce baking dishes by brushing the inside bottom and sides with clarified butter. Then, dust with bread crumbs. Place the excess bread crumbs in the mushrooms.

Evenly divide the mushrooms between the four dishes. Pour in eggs and place in a 350 degree oven until puffed and browned lightly, about 20 minutes. When done, top with grated parmesan and serve with velouté sauce.

For Velouté Sauce
Mix flour and butter and set aside. Bring chicken stock to a simmer. Add flour and butter, stirring constantly. Simmer for five minutes. Season with salt and pepper and serve.

GAME HEN WITH QUINCE BUTTER

[serves 4]

FOR THE GAME HEN
2 small cornish game hens
2 cups Cottage chicken stock *(page 167)*
¼ cup white table wine
1 shallot, sliced thin
2 carrots, peeled and chopped
1 tbsp. fresh thyme leaves, chopped fine
4 ounces butter, unsalted
salt and cracked pepper as needed
olive oil, extra virgin as needed

FOR THE QUINCE BUTTER
2 fresh quinces, peeled and cored
¼ cup honey, orange blossom
¼ cup brown sugar
2 cups champagne
4 ounces butter, unsalted and softened
course sea salt and cracked pepper as needed

Quinces are related to apples. They must be soaked in water with a touch of lemon juice or vinegar to keep from turning brown.

FOR THE GAME HEN
Split the birds in half. Generously season with salt and pepper. Drizzle a tablespoon of olive oil in a large sauté pan set over high heat. Add the game hens and brown on both sides. Remove the birds to a roasting pan.

Add shallots, carrots and thyme to the sauté pan. Sauté the vegetables for three to five minutes, stirring frequently. Add white wine and chicken stock. Melt butter into the liquid and pour over game hens. Cover the roasting pan with foil and place into a 375 degree oven for 20 to 30 minutes or until desired doneness. Serve with the quince butter.

FOR THE QUINCE BUTTER
Combine all ingredients in a sauce pot and bring to a simmer. Cook until the quinces are soft. Strain the quince and allow cooling. Reserve two or three tablespoons of the liquid reduction. Adjust the seasoning with salt and pepper.

In an upright electric mixer with a whip attachment, whisk the butter and quince together. Add the liquid reduction to the butter and mix well.

Place the butter on plastic wrap and roll it. Tie off the ends and place in freezer for two hours. To serve, slice thick medallions and place atop the Cornish game hens.

BUTTERSCOTCH CRÈME

[serves 4]

    1 ½ cups cream
    ⅓ cup brown sugar
    ¼ cup (or as desired) single malt scotch
    pinch of sea salt
    2 tbsp. cornstarch

In a heavy bottomed sauce pan, heat cream, brown sugar and scotch together. Lower the heat and bring to a slow simmer.

Dissolve the cornstarch with a touch of water. Whisk into the hot cream. Continuously stir until cream is very thick. Remove from the heat and transfer to a shallow pan. Cover and refrigerate at least four hours. Serve with fresh berries or chocolate shavings.

6 Course Chef's Winter Tasting Menu

First Course
Champagne and Gruyère Soup with Marjoram Croutons
Wine Pairing: 2006 Domaine Carneros Brut Vintage Cuvée, California

Second Course
Duck Confit Salad with Dried Cherries and Pomegranate Compote

Third Course
Steamed Mussels with Fresh Fennel and Pernod
Wine Pairing: 2008 Chappellet Chardonnay, California

Fourth Course
Potato Mousseline
Wine Pairing: 2004 Château Villa Bel-Air Graves, France

Fifth Course
Venison with Burgundy Wine and Juniper Berry Reduction
Wine Pairing: 2005 Serradenari Nebbiolo Langhe, Italy

Sixth Course
Crêpes with Grand Marnier, Toasted Pine Nuts and Candied Orange

CHAMPAGNE AND GRUYÈRE SOUP WITH MARJORAM CROUTONS

[serves 4]

1 quart Cottage chicken stock *(page 167)*
¼ cup champagne
½ cup heavy cream
½ cup Gruyère cheese, shredded
½ yellow onion, diced
1 stalk celery, diced

1 cup bread, dried and diced large
3 ounces butter, melted
3 ounces flour
1 tbsp. marjoram, chopped fine
sea salt and cracked pepper to taste

Heat 1 ounce of butter in large sauce pot. Add vegetables and sauté gently for 3 minutes or until tender. Add champagne and reduce by a quarter. Add chicken stock. Cover and simmer for 15 minutes.

Meanwhile, combine flour and two ounces of butter. Whisk into chicken stock. Cover again and reduce heat to low.

In a bowl, combine bread, marjoram and remaining butter. Toss well with a touch of sea salt and spread out on a baking tray. Bake in a preheated 400 degree oven for 7-10 minutes or until golden brown. Set aside.

Remove soup from heat and add the Gruyère cheese and cream. Stir frequently until thoroughly mixed. Adjust the seasoning with salt and pepper. Serve immediately with croutons on the side.

Duck Confit Salad with Dried Cherries and Pomegranate Compote

[serves 4]

For Duck Confit
4 duck legs
3 pound box kosher salt
pinch of cloves, ground
2 bay leaves, ground
¼ tsp. white pepper, ground
¼ tsp. dried orange peel, ground
2 pounds duck fat or unsalted butter, melted

For the Dried Cherry and Pomegranate Compote
¼ cup dried cherries, Michigan tart
¼ cup pomegranate seeds
½ shallot, diced fine
1 pint pomegranate juice
splash of cherry brandy
1 tbsp. white vinegar
¼ cup brown sugar
pinch of sea salt
1 tbsp. butter
2 tbsp. cornstarch
two handfuls of arugula

For Duck Confit
Mix together the cloves, bay leaves, white pepper and orange peel. Dust duck legs with spice mixture, evenly coating each leg. Place the legs in a cake pan. Cover the legs with kosher salt. Using your hand, tightly pack the salt and duck legs. Cover the pan and refrigerate 24 hours.

Thoroughly wash the duck legs. Dry with a clean kitchen towel and place in a small braising dish. Pour the melted duck fat or butter over the legs and place into a 200 degree oven for 6 to 8 hours or until the fat is clear and the legs are tender.

Allow duck legs to cool in the fat. Cover and refrigerate legs for 3 days. This is the ripening process. After ripening, soften the fat and duck legs by letting stand at room temperature for one hour. Remove duck legs to an oven proof dish and into a 400 degree oven until skin is golden and the meat heated through.

For the Dried Cherry and Pomegranate Compote
Combine all ingredients excluding the butter and cornstarch in a sauce pot. Bring mixture to boil over medium to high heat. Reduce to a slow simmer for 10 minutes.

Dissolve the cornstarch in water and whisk into the compote. Simmer for another 2 to 4 minutes. Finish the compote by stirring in the butter.

To complete the dish, bundle the arugula greens on a plate. Arrange the duck legs around the arugula greens. Dress the duck and greens with warm compote and serve.

STEAMED MUSSELS WITH FRESH FENNEL AND PERNOD

[serves 4]

2 dozen Prince Edward Island mussels, scrubbed
½ cup chardonnay
1 bulb fresh fennel, cored and shaved
2 cloves garlic, slivered
½ white onion, diced small
1 ounce plus clarified butter
1 ½ cups cream
⅛ cup Pernod
1 tsp. fresh thyme leaves, chopped fine
sea salt to taste

Place the scrubbed mussels in a pot. Add garlic, fresh thyme, wine and a touch of sea salt.   Bring to a simmer over high heat. Reduce heat to a low setting, cover pot and steam mussels until all the shells have opened or are starting to open. This usually takes no more than 5 to 7 minutes.

To make the sauce, add clarified butter to a sauce pan and heat over medium to high setting. Add onion and sauté until soft. Next, add fennel. Sauté for an additional three minutes. Do not brown the vegetables.

Add Pernod*. Reduce Pernod by half. Add a two ounce ladle of liquid from the steamed mussel pot. Finally, add cream. Reduce sauce until cream has thickened enough to coat the back of a spoon. Adjust the seasoning.

Drain mussels and arrange neatly in a serving bowl. Pour fennel sauce over the mussels. Garnish dish with bright green fennel fronds. Serve with crusty French bread and separate bowls for discarded shells.

*Please take care around open flames; Pernod is highly flammable.

Potato Mousseline

[serves 4]

3 yellow potatoes, peeled and sliced
3 egg yolks
3 egg whites
¼ cup cream
1 ounce butter
Gruyère cheese, shaved as needed
½ cup rice flour
1 tbsp. baking powder
salt and pepper as needed

Boil potato slices in salted water until very tender and easily mashed. Drain the cooked potatoes. Potatoes must be drained well of excess water.

Place potatoes in the bowl of an upright kitchen mixer. Fix bowl to unit with the whisk attachment. Turn the mixer on, increasing the speed to high. Process the potatoes until well mashed.

Pause mixer and add the egg yolks. Mix well and add cream, butter and rice flour. Adjust the seasoning and continue to mix until smooth. Transfer the potato dough to a large bowl. Wrap the bowl and refrigerate for at least two hours.

Using the kitchen mixer again, beat egg whites at a high speed to soft peaks. Add lemon juice and continue to beat until the peaks are stiff.

Fold the meringue into potato batter. Mix well and ladle or scoop mix into large soufflé cups. Place into a 375 degree oven and cook until golden brown and puffed, approximately 20 to 25 minutes.

Shave or shred Gruyère cheese over mousseline and serve at once.

VENISON WITH BURGUNDY WINE AND JUNIPER BERRY REDUCTION

[serves 4]

4 venison chops, 5 ounces each
1 shallot, chopped
6 juniper berries
1 clove garlic
½ cup burgundy wine
¼ cup dry gin
2 cups beef stock

2 ounces flour
1 ounce butter, melted
drizzle of olive oil
sea salt and cracked black pepper as needed

Heat olive oil in a large sauce pan over high heat. Add the venison chops and brown on both sides. Place chops on a roasting rack. Salt and pepper the meat and place in a 375 degree oven for 12 minutes (rare-medium rare) or longer for desired doneness. Be sure to allow the meat to rest at least ten minutes before serving.

Pulverize shallots, garlic and juniper berries in a food processor or mortar and pestle. Add contents to the sauté pan and return to medium heat. Sauté shallots, garlic and juniper berries for two minutes. Add wine and gin. Please note that gin is flammable.

Reduce the wine and gin by half and add beef stock. Simmer for 15 minutes.

Mix together butter and flour. Whisk this into the simmering sauce and stir frequently as it thickens. Simmer for an additional 3 to 5 minutes. Adjust the seasoning with salt and fresh cracked pepper. Strain the sauce through a fine mesh sieve over the rested venison chops. The dish is now ready to serve.

CRÊPES WITH GRAND MARNIER, TOASTED PINE NUTS AND CANDIED ORANGE

[serves 4]

FOR THE CRÊPES
1 cup all-purpose flour
2 tbsp. sugar
pinch of salt
2 eggs, cracked and whisked
¼ cup soda water
¾ cup milk, whole

FOR THE GRAND MARNIER SAUCE
1 ½ cup fresh squeezed orange juice
3 tbsp. honey

⅛ cup Grand Marnier
2 tbsp. butter, unsalted and softened
1 ½ tbsp. cornstarch
2 tbsp. candied orange peel, chopped fine
⅛ cup toasted pine nuts, salted

CANDIED ORANGE PEEL
3 orange peels, no pith (white flesh)
1 cup plus ¼ cup sugar
1 ¼ cup water

FOR THE CRÊPES
Combine all ingredients and mix well. Allow to chill for at least thirty minutes.

Heat a ten inch, non-stick sauté pan. Spray the pan with food release (ex. Pam®). Ladle four ounces of the batter into pan. Swirl pan to evenly distribute batter. Cook the crêpe until slightly brown. Turn crêpe over gently with a rubber spatula and, again, cook until browned.

FOR THE GRAND MARNIER SAUCE
Bring the orange juice, honey and Grand Marnier to a simmer. Dissolve the cornstarch with about two tablespoons water and whisk into simmering orange juice. Stir frequently and reduce heat to the lowest setting. Stir in butter.

Pour the sauce over the crêpes. Sprinkle each crêpe with toasted pine nuts and candied orange peel. Serve with whipped cream if desired.

FOR THE CANDIED ORANGE PEEL
Boil the orange peel five times for five minutes, changing the water each time. This will remove any of the bitter oils in the rind. Combine sugar, water and boiled orange peels. Bring the mixture to a simmer for 20 minutes or until the mixture has a visibly syrup-like consistency. Strain the liquid reserving the orange peel and the liquid separately. Allow the orange peel to cool at room temperature. This will take thirty minutes or more. Dredge the orange peel in sugar and then dice. It is now ready to serve.

6 Course Chef's Winter Tasting Menu

First Course
Hickory Smoked Onion Soup
Wine Pairing: 2009 Groth Sauvignon Blanc, California

Second Course
Pan Seared Goat Cheese with Micro-Greens and Poached Quail Egg

Third Course
Bouillabaisse Marseille with Saffron Broth and Garlic Rouille
Wine Pairing: 2009 Seghesio Fiano, California

Fourth Course
Potato and Taleggio Puffs
Wine Pairing: 2009 Château Puygueraud Côtes du Francs, France

Fifth Course
Pheasant Cassoulet
Wine Pairing: 2009 Evodia Old Vine Grenache, Spain

Sixth Course
Chambord and Custard "French Toast" with Burgundy Butter

HICKORY SMOKED ONION SOUP

[serves 4]

2 cups hickory wood chips	1 cup sherry, dry
2 yellow onions, peeled and halved	4 tbsp. cornstarch
1 quart beef stock	4 sliced French bread, large
2 cloves garlic, crushed	1 cup Gruyère cheese, shredded
1 tbsp. fresh thyme, chopped	4 tbsp. water
2 tbsp. olive oil	salt and pepper to taste

Begin by soaking the wood chips in water for 15 minutes. Strain the chips and wrap them in aluminum foil. With a fork, poke holes in foil. Set aside.

Heat an outdoor grill and place wood chips on the grill. Adjust heat to high and allow chips to smoke. Place onion halves on grill and smoke for 20 minutes. Remove onions and julienne. Set aside.

Add olive oil to a stock pot and heat over medium heat. Add onions and cook until caramelized in color. This takes about 20 minutes. Add sherry and reduce by half. Add beef stock, garlic and thyme. Cover and simmer for 15 minutes.

Meanwhile, combine the cornstarch and water. Whisk into the soup and simmer until slightly thickened.

Ladle soup into oven proof soup bowls. Fry 4 slices of French bread in butter until golden brown. Season with salt and pepper. Float one crouton in each bowl. Top with shredded Gruyère and place into a preheated 350 degree oven until cheese is melted. Serve immediately.

PAN SEARED GOAT CHEESE WITH MICRO-GREENS AND POACHED QUAIL EGG

[serves 4]

4 slices of chevre, 2 ounces each, frozen 24 hours
2 cracked eggs, whisked
¼ cup panko bread crumbs
½ cup canola oil
1 cup arugula micro-greens
4 pieces French bread, sliced
8 quail eggs
¼ cup white vinegar

1 tbsp. balsamic vinegar
2 tbsp. olive oil, extra virgin
1 ½ tsp. Dijon mustard
1 tsp. lavender honey
1 tsp. shallots, minced
salt and pepper to taste
2 ounces clarified butter

Cover and freeze the goat cheese slices overnight.

In a bowl, whisk the balsamic vinegar into the olive oil. Add shallots, honey and Dijon. Whisk until incorporated. Adjust seasoning with salt and pepper. Set aside.

Heat clarified butter in a sauté pan. Fry French bread pieces until golden brown on both sides. Season the toast with just a sprinkle of sea salt. Set croutons to the side.

Bring one quart of salted water to a boil. Add vinegar and reduce water to low. The water should be still.

With kitchen shears, carefully cut the top of the quail eggs. Stir the water and gently release the cracked egg white and yolk into the water. Poach for not more than three minutes. Remove eggs from the poaching water with a slotted kitchen spoon to the top of the toast. This is a delicate process that takes patience. Do not poach more than four eggs at a time.

Cover and freeze the goat cheese slices overnight. Heat canola oil to 400 degrees in a sauce pot. Meanwhile, toss the panko bread crumbs with just a drizzle of canola oil and set to the side.

Dip the frozen goat cheese slices in the whisked egg. Then, dip the slices in bread crumbs. Immerse goat cheese slices into hot oil. Fry until golden brown, season with salt and pepper and drain well on a clean kitchen towel.

To plate, place the quail egg and toast on a salad plate. Top with the arugula micro-greens. Serve the fried cheese just next to toast. Drizzle ingredients with vinaigrette and serve.

Bouillabaisse Marseille with Saffron Broth and Garlic Rouille

[serves 4]

For the Bouillabaisse
4 king crab claws
4 fresh jumbo prawns, shell on
4 jumbo sea scallops
4 cherrystone clams
8 mussels, scrubbed
8 ounce monkfish tail, cleaned and trimmed
1 cup white bordeaux
1 quart water
½ leek, washed and chopped
2 stalks celery, rough cut
1 carrot, rough cut
2 cloves garlic, smashed
1 tsp. orange peel

2 bay leaves
1 tsp. black peppercorns
1 tbsp. fresh thyme leaves, chopped fine
1 tsp. spanish saffron threads
Sea salt as needed
4 fresh French bread slices
2 tbsp. fresh parsley, chopped

For the Garlic Rouille
¼ cup mayonnaise
3 cloves garlic, minced to a paste
1 tsp. fresh lemon juice
sea salt, course as needed
dash of cayenne pepper

For the Bouillabaisse
Peel and devein shrimp. Place the shrimp shells in a large sauce pot. Next, peel the tough muscle off of the side of the scallops. Place mussel in with shrimp shells.

Add all of the ingredients, excluding the fish and shellfish, to the sauce pot. Bring ingredients to a slow simmer. Cover and cook for 30 to 40 minutes. Strain the liquid through a fine sieve. Adjust the taste with sea salt. Place strained liquid back into a sauce pot and return to medium heat. Bring to a simmer and reduce to low heat.

Add the mussels and clams. Poach until mussels and clams begin to open. Add remaining seafood and poach until all of the seafood is cooked, between 10 and 15 minutes. Be careful not to overcook the seafood.

Arrange seafood in a serving bowl, placing the bread pieces over the top of the seafood. Top this with chopped parsley and garlic rouille. Pour the hot broth over the bread and seafood and serve immediately with an empty bowl for shell discard.

For the Garlic Rouille
Combine all ingredients and serve.

POTATO AND TALEGGIO PUFFS

[serves 4]

1 yellow potato, peeled and chopped
½ shallot, diced fine
2 ounces Taleggio cheese, melted
1 cup all-purpose flour
1 egg, cracked and whisked
¼ cup soda water
3 tbsp. milk, whole
1 tbsp. baking powder
salt and cracked black pepper as needed
½ cup bread crumbs, fine
1 quart frying oil

FOR VELOUTÉ SAUCE
2 cups Cottage chicken stock *(page 167)*
2 ounces all-purpose flour
1 ounce clarified butter
salt and cracked white pepper as needed

Boil potato pieces in salted water until tender. Strain and allow potatoes to cool. Crumble potato pieces with your fingers; the crumbles should be large.

Add flour to a stainless steel bowl. Make a well in the center of the flour and add cracked eggs. Whisk the eggs and flour together. Add the soda water as needed to loosen batter. Add milk, shallot, and baking powder. Mix until smooth. Stir in cheese and adjust the taste with salt and pepper. Fold in the potato crumbles. Cover and refrigerate for at least two hours.

Heat the frying oil to 400 degrees. Using a scoop no larger than 1 ½ ounces, scoop a ball of potato batter into a pan of bread crumbs. Using a spoon, cover the batter with bread crumbs. Carefully pick up the ball and drop into hot oil. Fry until golden brown and puffy, approximately five minutes. Transfer the puffs to a cooling rack. Place the cooling rack on a baking sheet. Place the puffs in a 375 degree oven for ten minutes. Serve with velouté sauce.

FOR VELOUTÉ SAUCE
Combine the flour and butter and set aside.

Bring the chicken stock to a simmer. Whisk flour and butter together and then add to the simmering stock. Stir frequently as the sauce thickens. Simmer for 3 minutes and serve. Adjust seasoning with salt and ground pepper.

PHEASANT CASSOULET

[serves 4]

4 pheasant breasts, partial bone-in, 4 ounces
4 ounces Italian fennel sausage
5 ounces Cottage chicken stock *(page 167)*
½ leek, washed and diced
1 small carrot, peeled and diced medium
2 cloves garlic, slivered thin
1 tsp. fresh thyme, chopped fine

¼ cup chardonnay
1 cup white beans, cooked
½ cup cream
salt and cracked pepper as needed
drizzle of olive oil, extra virgin

Heat olive oil in a large sauté pan over high heat. Sear the pheasant breasts, browning them on both sides. Place breasts on a roasting pan with rack. Set aside.

Add sausage, leeks, carrots, garlic and fresh thyme to pan and return to high heat. Brown the sausage, stirring all contents frequently. Add wine, chicken stock, cream and beans. Transfer ingredients to a casserole dish. Place the cassoulet, loosely covered with foil, into a 400 degree oven for 30 to 40 minutes or until the liquid has thickened. Adjust the seasoning.

Season the pheasant breasts with salt and pepper. Place into oven and roast at 400 degrees for 7 to 10 minutes or until the meat is medium rare to medium. Allow the pheasant breasts to rest for 5 to 10 minutes after cooking.

To serve, spoon the cassoulet into four serving bowls. Slice the pheasant meat and serve on top of the beans.

CHAMBORD AND CUSTARD "FRENCH TOAST" WITH BURGUNDY BUTTER

[serves 4]

4 petite croissants
4 egg yolks
1 ¼ cups cream
½ cup plus 2 teaspoons sugar
¼ cup Chambord
1 ounce clarified butter

FOR THE BURGUNDY BUTTER
¼ cup burgundy wine
¼ cup sugar
2 ounces butter, unsalted and softened
2 tbsp. whipping cream

Score the croissants with a serrated knife and set aside.

Whisk together the egg yolks and sugar. Add Chambord and cream. Mix well.

Heat the clarified butter in a sauté pan on medium heat. Soak croissants in custard and place them in the pan. Pan-fry croissants until browned on each side. Move the croissants to a baking sheet lined with parchment paper. Sprinkle the croissants with the remaining two tablespoons of sugar and place them into a 350 degree oven for 10 minutes or until risen and firm. Serve immediately with sweet burgundy butter.

FOR THE BURGUNDY BUTTER
Combine the wine and sugar in a sauce pot. Reduce wine and sugar over low to medium heat until it forms a thick syrup. Remove from the heat and allow to cool.

Whip the butter and cream in an upright mixer. Pour in the burgundy syrup and mix well. Cover and refrigerate butter for thirty minutes and serve.

SPRING

6 Course Chef's Spring Tasting Menu

First Course
Wild Mushroom Bisque with Fried Leeks and Sherry
Wine Pairing: 2007 Ken Forrester Chenin Blanc, Stellenbosch - South Africa

Second Course
Asparagus Bundles Wrapped in Proscuitto with Hollandaise

Third Course
Potato Crusted Steelhead Trout with Capers and Brown Butter
Wine Pairing: 2007 Chateau Montelana Chardonnay, Napa Valley

Fourth Course
Pommes Anna with White Truffle Oil
Wine Pairing: 2004 Barolo Conca Renato Ratti, Italy

Fifth Course
Petite Lamb Loin Chop Puttanesca
Wine Pairing: 2008 Volver Tempranillo, Spain

Sixth Course
Lemon Curd

WILD MUSHROOM BISQUE WITH FRIED LEEKS AND SHERRY

[serves 4]

FOR THE BISQUE
5 ounces fresh morels, cleaned
4 cloves garlic, crushed
1 quart Cottage chicken stock *(page 167)*
1 tbsp. fresh thyme, chopped fine
2 ounces butter, melted
3 ounces all-purpose flour
⅛ cup dry sherry
½ cup heavy whipping cream
drizzle of extra virgin olive oil
salt and pepper to taste

FOR THE LEEKS
½ cup leeks, washed and julienned fine
3 tbsp. cornstarch
sea salt to taste
1 cup frying oil

FOR THE BISQUE
In a large sauce pot, heat the olive oil and add garlic and morels. Gently sauté until soft. Add fresh thyme and sherry. Reduce by half and add the chicken stock. Cover and simmer for 30 minutes.

Combine flour and butter. Add to the simmering stock. Stir frequently and cook for 5 additional minutes. Add cream and serve immediately with fried leeks.

FOR THE LEEKS
Heat frying oil to 400 degrees in a sauce pot. Toss the leeks and cornstarch, making sure the leeks are evenly coated. Drop coated leeks in the hot oil and fry until golden brown. Season to taste and serve.

Missouri mushroom season can be hit or miss depending on the weather. Use the kind that you like or what is currently available. This recipe calls for morels. As with all wild mushrooms, source them from trusted and educated gatherers. Prior to preparation, soak mushrooms in cold and salted water for 30 minutes before rinsing and straining.

Asparagus Bundles Wrapped in Proscuitto with Hollandaise

[serves 4]

20 spears fresh asparagus
4 slices prosciutto, sliced thin
2 ounces olive oil
cracked black pepper to taste

Hollandaise sauce
4 egg yolks
¼ cup butter, unsalted and clarified
3 tbsp. chardonnay, dry
2 tbsp. lemon juice, freshly squeezed
sea salt and ground black pepper to taste

Cut off the bottom inch of the asparagus. Discard the ends. Bring a pot of seasoned fresh water to a boil. Add the asparagus spears. Boil for 2 minutes. Spears will be bright green and very crispy. Immerse spears in ice water until fully cooled. Strain asparagus and set aside.

On a clean, flat surface, lay out a slice of prosciutto vertically. Season the prosciutto with cracked black pepper. Lay 5 asparagus spears horizontally across bottom of prosciutto slices. Roll up the prosciutto and place on a plate. Repeat this process for the remaining three guests.

Heat the olive oil in a sauté pan until very hot. Add the asparagus bundles and fry, turning frequently, until golden brown and crispy. Serve immediately with hollandaise sauce.

For Sauce
In a sauce pot, boil 1 quart of water. In a stainless steel bowl, whisk egg yolks. Temper the yolks by adding one ounce of the boiling water while whisking vigorously. Place bowl over water pot and stir until the yolks thicken. Slowly whisk in butter. Add remaining ingredients, stirring constantly. Adjust seasoning with ground pepper and sea salt.

Potato Crusted Steelhead Trout with Capers and Brown Butter

[serves 4]

4 fresh steelhead trout fillets, skinned, 5 ounce fillets
1 Yukon gold potato, sliced thin
3 cloves of fresh garlic, slivered
1 ounce clarified butter
2 tbsp. whole butter, unsalted
1 tbsp. fresh lemon juice
¼ cup Cottage chicken stock *(page 167)*

2 tbsp. capers
1 small shallot, diced
4 fluffy sprigs of curly parsley
sea salt to taste
ground black pepper to taste

Season trout fillets with salt and cracked pepper. Slice potato paper thin. This is best accomplished on a mandoline. Shingle the potato slices, covering the top of the fillets.

Heat the clarified butter to searing hot. Place the fish fillets in the pan, potatoes down. Pan-fry until potatoes are golden brown and crispy. Remove to a roasting tray. Season the top of the fish with sea salt. Place fish into a 375 degree oven to finish cooking. This will take no more than 7 to 10 minutes.

Add whole butter to the pan and return to medium heat. Heat the butter until it browns. Add shallots and garlic and cook until soft. Add chicken stock and reduce by half. Add lemon juice and, again, reduce by half. Add capers and adjust the seasoning with salt and pepper.

Remove fish from oven to a serving tray. Pour sauce over the fish and serve with fresh parsley. The parsley is not a garnish but an element of the dish to be enjoyed.

Pommes Anna with White Truffle Oil

[serves 4]

3 Yukon gold potatoes, sliced to $\frac{1}{16}$ in.
2 ounces clarified butter
sea salt as needed
1 tbsp. fresh thyme leaves, chopped fine
drizzle of white truffle oil

Pour butter into a non-stick and oven-proof 7 in. sauté pan. Shingle the potatoes in a circular pattern to the center of the pan. Season with salt and sprinkle thyme leaves evenly.

Pan-fry the potatoes over medium to high heat until golden brown. Place pan into a 400 degree oven and cook until potatoes are soft and the bottom crispy. Remove and carefully invert the pan to a large plate. Display the crispy brown side up. Cut into quarters and drizzle with white truffle oil. Serve immediately.

PETITE LAMB LOIN CHOP PUTTANESCA

[serves 4]

4 lamb loin chops, 3 to 5 ounces
2 tomatoes, peeled, seeded and diced
2 cloves garlic, slivered
1 tbsp. shallots, minced
12 calamata olives, pitted
2 tbsp. capers
splash of red table wine
½ tsp. lemon zest
pinch of crushed red pepper

sea salt as needed
pinch of sugar
½ tsp. tomato paste
1 fillet of anchovy, chopped
1 ounce olive oil
fresh mint, optional

Drizzle olive oil in a sauté pan and place on high heat. Add lamb chops and brown on both sides. Transfer lamb to a baking tray lined with a roasting rack. Place into a 375 degree oven and roast until medium rare, 15 minutes, or to desired temperature.

Add garlic and shallots to the pan and sauté until tender. Add tomatoes, wine, olives and capers. Simmer until sauce has thickened, about 7 minutes. Add remaining ingredients and stir well. Serve over the rested lamb chops with fresh mint if desired.

LEMON CURD

[serves 4]

    5 egg yolks
    ¼ cup sugar
    1 tsp. butter, unsalted and softened
    juice from 2 fresh lemons
    pinch of sea salt
    pinch of lemon zest
    4 lady finger cookies

Fill a double boiler with water a quarter of its volume. Bring the water to just under a boil.

Combine the eggs and sugar in the top pan of the double boiler. Whisk well and temper the eggs with an ounce of the hot water. Whisk well and then place the pan on top of the water pot. Whisk vigorously until the eggs are light and thick. This will take 7 to 10 minutes.

Add lemon juice, zest and salt. Continue to cook and whisk until very thick. Remove from heat and continue to rapidly whisk. This will cool the curd quickly.

Add butter and mix well. Serve immediately with lady fingers, or cover and refrigerate for later use.

6 Course Chef's Spring Tasting Menu

First Course
Pistou Soup with Mascarpone Cheese
Wine Pairing: 2007 Chalk Hill North Slope Pinot Gris, Sonoma

Second Course
Caramelized Artichokes and Pancetta Ragoût
Served with Petite Belgium Endive

Third Course
Aiguillettes of Red Snapper with Ginger Beurre Blanc and Young Peas
Wine Pairing: 2009 Damilano Arneis Langhe, Italy

Fourth Course
Asparagus and Spring Leek Frittata
Wine Pairing: 2008 Fritz Pinot Noir, Russian River Valley

Fifth Course
Tournedos of Beef with Béarnaise
Wine Pairing: 2007 Januik Champoux Vineyard Horse Heaven Hills
Cabernet Sauvignon, Washington State

Sixth Course
Crème Brûlée with Strawberries

PISTOU SOUP WITH MASCARPONE CHEESE

[serves 4]

1 pint Cottage chicken stock *(page 167)*
1 cup heavy cream
4 ounces basil, coarsely chopped
2 ounces pine nuts, toasted
2 cloves of garlic, crushed
4 ounces mascarpone cheese, melted
1 tbsp. lemon juice, fresh squeezed

drizzle of olive oil, extra virgin
2 ounces flour
1 ounce butter, unsalted and melted
Sea salt and cracked pepper to taste

Bring the chicken stock to a simmer. Mix flour and butter together. Add flour and butter to the simmering chicken stock. Simmer for 2 to 4 minutes, then chill.

In a food processor, combine the thickened chicken stock, cream, basil, pine nuts, garlic and lemon juice. Purée and chill for 1 hour. Season to taste and drizzle with olive oil. Serve immediately with warm mascarpone cheese.

CARAMELIZED ARTICHOKES AND PANCETTA RAGOÛT

[serves 4]

2 artichokes, jumbo
8 pearl onions, peeled
6 cloves garlic, roasted
3 ounces pancetta ham, diced
¼ cup white beans, cooked
1 tsp. fresh rosemary, chopped fine
1 fresh bay leaf
1 cup Cottage chicken stock *(page 167)*
¼ cup white table wine

1 tsp. cornstarch
pinch of sugar
course sea salt as needed
fresh ground pepper as needed
dash of white vinegar
drizzle of balsamic vinegar
drizzle of olive oil, extra virgin
8 Belgian endive spears, washed

Prepare the artichokes by cutting the top halves off. Place in a pot of water seasoned with salt and a dash of white vinegar. Simmer until tender, about 20 minutes. Strain artichokes and allow them to cool. Remove all of the tough outer leaves and discard. Remove artichoke carefully with a spoon or melon baller. Trim the fibrous strands off of the stem. Cut the cleaned artichokes in quarters and set aside.

Render pancetta ham in an oven-proof sauce pot over medium heat. Cook the pancetta until it has a crispy exterior. Remove from pan with slotted spoon and drain on a clean paper towel. Set the pancetta to the side.

Halve the onions and add them to the sauce pan. Add the artichokes and sauté until both the artichokes and onions are caramelized and golden in color. Remove and set aside.

To the onions and artichokes, add white beans, roasted garlic, bay leaf and chopped rosemary. Continue to sauté turning all ingredients well. Add the white wine. Simmer until wine is reduced by half. Add chicken stock and return to a simmer.

Dissolve the cornstarch in a bit of water. Whisk cornstarch and water into the simmering ragoût. Continue to simmer until the ragoût has thickened. Adjust taste with sugar, salt and cracked pepper.

Arrange two spears of Belgian endive on a plate. Drizzle the leaves with olive oil and balsamic vinegar. Spoon the ragoût over the endive leaves. Sprinkle the crispy pancetta over the top and serve with warm bread.

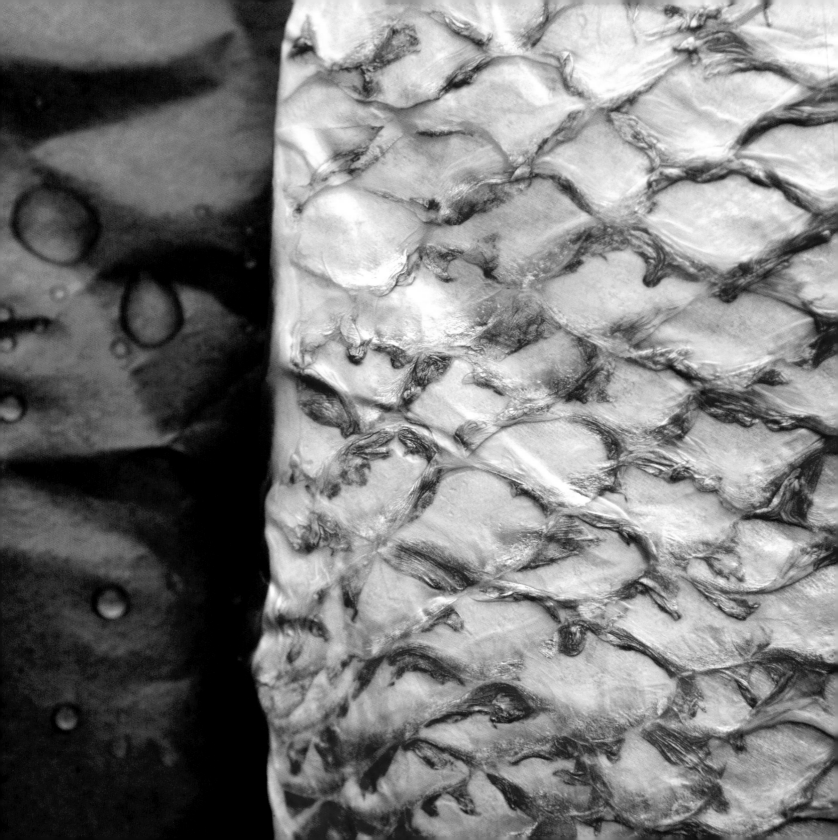

AIGUILLETTES OF RED SNAPPER WITH GINGER BEURRE BLANC AND YOUNG PEAS

[serves 4]

4 fillets of Florida red snapper, skinned and boned, 5 ounces each
dusting of rice flour
3 ounces fresh ginger, sliced
1 shallot, sliced
1 cup fresh peas
3 tbsp. rice vinegar
3 tbsp. white table wine
3 tbsp. water
2 tbsp. sugar
3 tbsp. whole butter, unsalted
¼ cup cream
¼ cup clarified butter
sea salt and ground white pepper to taste

In a sauce pan, combine ginger, shallots, vinegar, white wine, sugar and water. Bring to a slow simmer until a tablespoon of liquid remains. At this point, add cream and simmer until the cream starts to thicken. Strain cream through a fine mesh sieve and discard the ginger and onions. Add the peas and keep the cream warm. Set aside.

Heat clarified butter in a sauté pan. Dust the fillets of fish in rice flour. Pan-fry the fillets until golden brown and flaky. Transfer to a serving platter and arrange neatly. Sprinkle with salt and pepper.

Return cream to medium heat and whisk in the softened whole butter. Adjust taste with salt and pepper and serve immediately over red snapper fillets.

Asparagus and Spring Leek Frittata

[serves 4]

  6 whole eggs, cracked and whisked
  1 bundle fresh asparagus
  1 fresh leek, washed and sliced
  drizzle of olive oil, extra virgin
  1 tbsp. mascarpone cheese, melted
  2 cloves fresh garlic, minced
  dusting of fine bread crumbs
  sea salt as needed
  cracked pepper to taste
  romano cheese, freshly grated, as needed

Prepare asparagus by cutting and discarding the bottom quarter of the bunch. Asparagus ends can be woody and undesirable. Thinly slice remaining asparagus and set aside.

Add a drizzle of olive oil into a sauté pan. Add leeks and garlic. Sauté at a medium setting until the vegetables are softened. Set aside to cool.

Whisk eggs with the melted mascarpone cheese. Adjust the seasoning with salt and cracked pepper.

Oil an oven proof 7 in. casserole dish with olive oil. Dust the inside with bread crumbs. Line the bottom of dish with leeks and garlic. Layer sliced asparagus on top of the leeks. Pour in eggs and place into a 350 degree oven for 30 minutes or until firm. Serve at once with grated Romano cheese.

TOURNEDOS OF BEEF WITH BÉARNAISE

[serves 4]

  1 ½ lbs. beef tenderloin
  3 cloves garlic
  3 fresh rosemary sprigs, 1 in. length
  5 egg yolks
  4 ounces clarified butter
  1 tsp. tarragon vinegar
  splash of chardonnay
  sea salt to taste
  fresh ground black pepper as needed

Be sure the beef has been trimmed of any excess fat. Cut three incisions evenly spaced and an inch deep on the top of the tenderloin. Stuff one garlic clove and one sprig of rosemary in each hole.

Drizzle a bit of clarified butter in a sauté pan over high heat. Sear beef, browning it on all sides. Season the beef well with sea salt and ground pepper. Place on a roasting rack and into a preheated 375 degree oven until desired doneness. It will take approximately 20 to 30 minutes for a medium rare to medium temperature.

In a double boiler, whisk the egg yolks with an ounce of hot water from the bottom pan. This will temper the eggs. Return the top pan to the double boiler and whisk egg yolks vigorously until they are pale in color and thickening. Slowly whisk in the clarified butter. Add vinegar and wine. This may thin out the sauce. If it does, continue whisking over the double boiler until sauce will firmly hold to the back of a spoon. Add salt and cracked pepper to your liking.

Remove and discard the rosemary sprigs from the beef. Slice the tenderloin into medallions and neatly arrange on a serving tray. Serve immediately with béarnaise sauce on the side or poured over the beef.

Crème Brûlée with Strawberries

[serves 4]

    1 pint heavy cream, heated
    5 egg yolks
    1 whole egg, cracked
    ¾ cup of sugar, plus ¼ cup for dusting
    pinch of salt
    ¼ tsp. vanilla
    8 fresh strawberries, stemmed and halved
    drizzle of lavender honey

Whisk egg yolks, egg, sugar, salt and vanilla together in a stainless steel bowl. Temper eggs with one ounce hot cream (add cream to the eggs, whisking vigorously). Add remaining cream and stir well.

Skim the accumulated foam off the top of the custard with a spoon. Evenly distribute the custard base to 4 to 6 ounce ramekins. Place the ramekins in a roasting pan and fill the roasting pan with very hot water, to a level half way up the side of the ramekins. Place in a 350 degree oven for 20 to 30 minutes or until the custards are firm. Refrigerate custards for at least 3 hours.

Dust the tops of the chilled custards with sugar. Shake off excess sugar. Using a crème brûlée torch, flambé the sugared tops until caramelized.

In a bowl, toss strawberries with lavender honey. Serve the berries with the crème brûlée.

6 Course Chef's Spring Tasting Menu

First Course
Asparagus Soup with Toasted Pistachios and Spring Leeks
Wine Pairing: 2008 Huber Grüner Veltliner Obere Steigen, Austria

Second Course
Baby Arugula Dressed in Extra Virgin Olive Oil, Sea Salt and Lemon
Served in Romano Crêpe

Third Course
Escargot with Plugra Garlic Butter and Croissant Point
Wine Pairing: 2005 Rombauer Chardonnay, Carneros

Fourth Course
Potato and Spring Ramp Gratin
Wine Pairing: 2006 Marimar Mas Cavalls Pinot Noir, Sonoma

Fifth Course
Rabbit Ragoût with Pappardelle Pasta and Shaved Asiago
Wine Pairing: 2006 Renato Ratti Barolo Marcenasco, Italy

Sixth Course
Rhubarb Pots de Crème

Asparagus Soup with Toasted Pistachios and Spring Leeks

[serves 4]

 1 quart Cottage chicken stock *(page 167)*
 1 dozen purple asparagus tips, thinly sliced
 ½ leek, washed and diced
 ⅛ cup pistachios, crushed and toasted
 2 cloves fresh garlic, slivered
 2 ounces clarified butter
 1 tbsp. lemon juice
 2 ounces flour
 ½ cup cream
 sea salt as needed
 fresh ground black pepper as needed

In a bowl, combine 1ounce of butter and flour. Stir the mixture until incorporated and set aside.

Over a medium stovetop heat setting, bring the chicken stock to a simmer. Whisk in the flour and butter mixture. Simmer until the stock has thickened. Stir in the cream and reduce the heat to low.

Pour the remaining 1 ounce of butter into a sauté pan. Heat butter over medium heat and add the garlic and leeks. Sauté until leeks are soft. Add purple asparagus and sauté for no more than 2 or 3 minutes. Add lemon juice and adjust the taste with salt and pepper.

Transfer the sautéed asparagus and leeks into the thickened chicken stock. Stir well and serve immediately, garnishing with the toasted pistachios

Baby Arugula Dressed in Extra Virgin Olive Oil, Sea Salt and Lemon

[serves 4]

For the Crêpes
1 cup all-purpose flour
2 eggs, cracked
pinch of sea salt
1 tsp. sugar
2 ounces Romano cheese, shredded
¾ cup sparkling water
¾ cup milk, whole

For the Lemon Vinaigrette and Arugula
juice from 1 plump lemon
1 tbsp. rice wine vinegar, seasoned
½ tsp. lemon zest
1 tbsp. clover honey
sea salt, course, as needed
½ tsp. lemon balm, finely chopped
drizzle of walnut oil
8 ounces baby arugula

For the Crêpes
Combine all ingredients and mix until smooth. Allow to rest for thirty minutes at room temperature prior to use.

Heat a 10 in. non-stick skillet on medium. Spray pan with pan release (Pam®). Ladle 4 ounces of the batter into the pan. Move the pan around to evenly coat. Cook until bottom side of crêpe is brown. Remove and set on a plate. Repeat this process for remaining batter.   Upon completion, keep the sauté pan warm for later use.

For the Lemon Vinaigrette and Arugula
Combine all ingredients except arugula and whisk well. Toss arugula with dressing. Reheat the crêpe pan and spray with pan release. Brown the uncooked side of the crêpe. When browned, remove and wrap with arugula. Serve at once.

Escargot with Plugra Garlic Butter and Croissant Point

[serves 4]

16 Helix snails, rinsed and shelled
3 cloves garlic, slivered thin
1 tsp. curly parsley, chopped fine
1 tbsp. fresh lemon juice
2 ounces European-style butter, unsalted
2 tbsp. clarified butter
¾ cup cream
sea salt to taste
cracked black pepper, as needed
2 miniature croissants, halved and toasted

Heat clarified butter in a sauce pan over medium- high heat. Add garlic and sauté until soft but not brown. Remove from heat and allow to cool for a couple of minutes. Add snails and lemon juice. Return to heat and bring to a simmer. Add cream and continue reducing until the cream starts to thicken. Soften butter and add to cream sauce. Adjust the taste with salt and pepper. Stir in parsley and serve immediately with the toasted croissant points.

POTATO AND SPRING RAMP GRATIN

[serves 4]

    6 spring ramps, washed and trimmed
    1 yellow potato, sliced to ³⁄₁₆ in.
    ½ cup gouda, shredded
    1 pint cream
    3 egg yolks
    pinch of cardamom
    sea salt as needed
    cracked black pepper as needed
    sprinkle of fine bread crumbs

Spring ramps are available at some area gourmet stores for a very short window, in April to May. These onion-like delicacies have sweetly pungent notes of garlic and leeks.

Cut the ramps in half (length). Season with salt and cracked pepper and set aside.

Heat cream and cardamom to just under a simmer. Remove from heat and add shredded cheese. Stir frequently to evenly melt the cheese.

Whisk egg yolks in a separate bowl. Add an ounce or two of the hot cream to the yolks, whisking vigorously. Add the egg yolks to the cream sauce. Stir sauce frequently over low heat for 5 to 7 minutes. The sauce will start to thicken. Adjust the seasoning with salt and pepper. Remove sauce from heat and put aside for later use.

Layer the sliced potatoes in a deep 5 1/5 in. soufflé dish. Lightly season the potatoes with salt. Next, layer the ramps. Pour the cream sauce over ramps and potatoes. Top with bread crumbs, cover with foil and place into a 350 degree oven. Bake the gratin for 40 minutes or until the potatoes are tender.

Turn the oven setting to 'broil'. Remove the foil from potatoes. Toast the top of the gratin until golden. Serve immediately.

RABBIT RAGOÛT WITH PAPPARDELLE PASTA AND SHAVED ASIAGO

[serves 4]

2 each of fresh rabbit thighs and legs
3 strips Applewood smoked bacon, diced
1 sweet onion, diced large
2 young carrots, sliced large
¼ cup fava beans, shelled
1 cup burgundy wine
1 pint beef stock
1 cup water
2 cloves garlic, crushed
1 tbsp. fresh thyme leaves, chopped fine
1 bay leaf

1 ounce chocolate, bittersweet
1 ounce clarified butter
2 tbsp. whole butter, unsalted
sea salt, course, as needed
cracked black pepper as needed
1 wedge Asiago cheese
6 ounces fresh egg noodles
dusting of flour

Render bacon until crispy in a sauté pan over high heat; remove from the pan using a slotted kitchen spoon. Drain bacon on a plate lined with a clean paper towel. Add the clarified butter to the pan and return to heat. Dust the rabbit with flour and place in pan. Pan-fry the rabbit until browned on all sides. Remove to an oven proof casserole dish.

Add onions, carrots and garlic to pan. Give the vegetables a couple of turns with your kitchen spoon. Add red wine, beef stock, chocolate, fresh thyme, water and bay leaf. Adjust the seasoning with salt and pepper. Stir well to ensure chocolate is evenly incorporated. Pour the liquid over rabbit. Cover rabbit with foil and place in a 325 degree oven for one hour or until meat is tender and liquid thickened. Finish the rabbit by stirring in the whole butter. Keep warm.

Boil a pot of salted water. Add pasta and fava beans. Cook until tender. Strain and add to the rabbit ragoût. Fold gently and present in a large bowl. Top the dish by crumbling the bacon. Using a carrot peeler, shave the Asiago off of the wedge. It is ready to be enjoyed.

RHUBARB POTS DE CRÈME

[serves 4]

    2 stalks of rhubarb, washed and chopped fine
    1 pint cream
    5 egg yolks
    1 whole egg, cracked
    1 cup sugar
    2 tsp. Chambord
    pinch of sea salt

Heat the cream and rhubarb together and simmer until rhubarb is very tender. Strain and push through a sieve.

Whisk the egg yolks, whole egg and sugar. Temper the eggs with a bit of the hot cream. Add the eggs to the cream and whisk well. Stir in Chambord and salt. Cover and refrigerate for at least three hours.

Skim the top of the custard base. Evenly divide custard to four custard dishes. Place in a water bath and into a 350 degree oven for 20 to 30 minutes or until custard is firm. Remove and refrigerate for 2 to 3 hours. Serve with whipped cream.

SUMMER

6 Course Chef's Summer Tasting Menu

First Course
Lobster Bisque with Poached Lobster Meat
Wine Pairing: 2009 Copain Viognier, California

Second Course
Golden and Ruby Beet Salad Alsace
with Toasted Shallots and Parmesan Crisp

Third Course
Alaskan Coho Salmon en Papillote with Lemon, Capers and Tomatoes
Wine Pairing: 2009 Domaines Paul Mas Picpoul de Pinet, France

Fourth Course
Missouri Chanterelle Risotto
Wine Pairing: 2007 Barons de Rothschild, Bordeaux Reserve, France

Fifth Course
Smoked Duck Cannelloni with Brown Butter and Sage
Wine Pairing: 2007 Gundlach Bundschu Pinot Noir, Sonoma

Sixth Course
Kahlúa and Chocolate Hot Pots with Fresh Raspberries

LOBSTER BISQUE WITH POACHED LOBSTER MEAT

[serves 4]

2 lobsters, live
¼ cup leeks, roughly chopped
1 carrot, peeled and chopped
2 cloves garlic, chopped
1 tbsp. tomato paste
¼ cup chardonnay
1 ½ quarts water, plus 1 qt. for poaching
1 cup heavy whipping cream

3 ounces all-purpose flour
2 ounces butter, melted
1 bay leaf
1 tsp. black peppercorns, cracked
1 tsp. dried orange peel
sea salt to taste

Place the live lobster on a flat surface. Insert a chef's knife into the head just behind the eyes. This will quickly put your lobsters to rest. Remove and refrigerate the tails and claws.

Rinse out the interior cavity of the lobster heads and put them into a soup pot. Add wine, leeks, garlic and carrot. Simmer over medium heat until half of the wine has reduced. Add water, tomato paste, bay leaf, black peppercorns and orange peel. Cover and simmer for one hour.

Meanwhile, bring 1 quart of salted water to a boil. Add the reserved lobster tails and claws. Simmer for 10 to 12 minutes or until lobster meat is cooked to desired doneness. Set aside and allow to cool. When cool, remove meat and chop coarsely. Sprinkle with a bit of sea salt and set aside.

Mix together flour and melted butter. Set aside. Strain the lobster stock. Return to heat and bring to a boil. Whisk in flour and butter mixture. Reduce heat and allow the bisque to simmer for 15 minutes or until thickened. Add cream and season to taste with sea salt.

Equally divide the reserved lobster meat between four soup bowls. Pour the hot bisque over the lobster meat and serve immediately.

Golden and Ruby Beet Salad Alsace with Toasted Shallots and Parmesan Crisp

[serves 4]

6 baby red beets, trimmed and washed
6 baby yellow beets, trimmed and washed
1 tbsp. fresh thyme leaves, chopped
3 tbsp. shallots, diced small
4 tbsp. olive oil
2 tbsp. balsamic vinegar
1 tbsp. brown sugar

¼ cup Parmesan cheese, grated
2 tbsp. cornstarch
3 tbsp. water
cracked pepper and sea salt to taste
4 ounces assorted baby lettuce leaves, washed

Place beets in separate pots, each filled with water and seasoned. This will keep the beets from coloring one another. Boil the beets until they are soft, approximately 20 to 30 minutes. Strain and run under cold water. Peel the skins and discard. Halve beets and place into two separate bowls. Set aside.

In a small sauce pot, add olive oil and heat over high temperature. Add shallots and toast until golden brown. Remove from heat and allow to cool. Add balsamic vinegar and honey. Drizzle a bit of the vinaigrette over both red and yellow beets. Sprinkle chopped, fresh thyme over beets and combine. Set aside.

On a baking tray lined with a non-stick mat, arrange grated cheese in thin circles. Place into a preheated 400 degree oven for 7 to 10 minutes or until cheese circles are golden brown. Carefully remove cheese crisps with a spatula and place on a paper towel or clean cloth.

Equally divide and arrange beets on a plate. Top with cleaned baby lettuces. Drizzle remaining vinaigrette over salad. Finish with a cheese crisp and serve.

Alaskan Coho Salmon en Papillote with Lemon, Capers and Tomatoes

[serves 4]

8 circles of 10 in. parchment paper circles
4 fresh salmon fillets, 5 ounce pieces
2 fresh tomatoes, diced
2 ounces capers, drained
2 cloves fresh garlic, crushed
1 shallot, minced
2 tbsp. butter, unsalted
salt and pepper to taste
olive oil, extra virgin, as needed

Drizzle olive oil in a small sauce pot. Add shallots and garlic and gently sauté until soft but not brown. Add tomatoes and capers and bring to a simmer. Add butter and simmer for an additional 3-5 minutes. Remove and set aside.

Arrange the salmon fillets on four of the paper circles. Sprinkle with salt and pepper. Ladle tomato sauce over the salmon and place remaining parchment circles on top. Fold to seal the pouches. Place in a preheated 375 degree oven and bake for 7 to 10 minutes or until desired temperature.

Missouri Chanterelle Risotto

[serves 4]

        5 ounces chanterelles, washed and trimmed
        1 shallot, minced
        2 cloves garlic, minced
        ½ pound arborio rice
        1 quart Cottage chicken stock, hot *(page 167)*
        2 ounces clarified butter
        sea salt as needed
        cracked pepper as needed
        2 tbsp. Parmesan cheese, grated

In a sauce pot, heat clarified butter over medium to high heat. Add shallots and garlic. Sauté the onions and garlic until soft. Add rice and chanterelles and continue to sauté for 1 minute. Add a cup of hot chicken stock to the rice. Stir frequently with a wooden spoon until most of the liquid has been absorbed. Add another half cup of the stock and continue stirring. Repeat this process until the rice is creamy and tender. Adjust seasoning with salt and cracked pepper. Serve with freshly grated parmesan cheese.

Smoked Duck Cannelloni with Brown Butter and Sage

[serves 4]

For the Filling
½ duck, fresh white 1 lb. Peking
2 shallots, peeled and halved
2 carrots, peeled and chopped
3 cups Cottage chicken stock *(page 167)*
½ pound butter, unsalted
2 bay leaves
2 cloves, whole
6 sprigs of fresh thyme
6 black peppercorns
½ tsp. orange peel, dried
2 tbsp. mayonnaise
2 tbsp. bread crumbs, fine
2 stalks celery, diced fine
Sea salt to taste
6" x 6" cheese cloth
twine, as needed
1 lb. hickory chips, soaked in water

For the Brown Butter Sauce
1 tbsp. fresh sage, chopped fine
¾ cup cream
¼ cup whole milk
¼ cup Cottage chicken stock *(page 167)*
1 ounce butter, unsalted
1 ½ ounce all-purpose flour
¼ yellow onion, diced fine
fresh ground white pepper as needed
sea salt to taste

For the Assembly and Finish
8 fresh pasta sheets, 6" x 6"

Heat chicken stock in a sauce pan. Add butter, shallots and carrots. Simmer on low for 15 minutes.

Securely wrap the fresh thyme, bay leaves, black peppercorns, cloves and dried orange peel in cheesecloth. Tie the bouquet with twine. Add to chicken stock.

Salt and pepper duck inside and out. Place into a deep roasting pan. Pour chicken stock and vegetables over duck. Wrap with foil and place into a 375 degree oven. Braise the duck for two hours or until tender.

Wrap hickory chips in aluminum foil. Using a fork, poke holes in the foil.

Heat an outdoor grill at the high setting. Place wrapped hickory chips on the grill and allow a good smoke to develop. This may take as much as 30 minutes.

Very carefully place the duck on a small baking sheet. Discard the braising liquid. Place duck onto grill and close the lid. Smoke duck for ten minutes. Remove and allow duck to cool. *(continued on next page)*

Separate duck meat from the bone. Discard bones and excess fat or gristle.

In a stainless steel bowl, shred duck meat with your hands. Add celery, mayonnaise and bread crumbs. Mix well and adjust the seasoning. Cover and refrigerate for later use.

FOR THE BROWN BUTTER SAUCE
Brown the butter in a sauce pan over a high heat setting. Stir butter frequently. When butter is golden brown, add onions and sauté until soft. Add flour and stir well. Next, add chicken stock, cream and milk. Turn the heat setting to low and allow to gently simmer until thickened. Stir in sage and adjust the seasoning. Keep warm.

FOR THE ASSEMBLY
Bring a pot of salted water to a rolling boil. Add the pasta and cook for 7 to 10 minutes or until tender. Chill the pasta in ice water.

Roll each pasta sheet with the smoked duck filling. Continue this process through completion. Place the cannelloni in a baking dish. Pour brown butter sauce over the cannelloni. Cover the dish with foil and place into a 350 degree oven. Bake for 20 minutes and serve.

Kahlûa and Chocolate Hot Pots with Fresh Raspberries

[serves 4]

FOR THE CAKE BATTER
¼ pound butter, unsalted and melted
4 ounces chocolate, bittersweet chips
2 ounces Kahlûa
3 eggs, cracked
2 ounces flour
⅛ cup sugar
1 tbsp. cocoa powder
1 tsp. baking powder
dash of sea salt

FOR THE CHOCOLATE GANACHE
¼ cup cream
2 ounces chocolate, bittersweet
2 tbsp. Kahlûa

Add the chocolate to the warm melted butter. Mix melting chocolate and butter well. Set aside.

Vigorously beat eggs, Kahlûa and sugar until eggs are pale in color and frothy. Stir in the chocolate and butter and mix completely.

Sift together all dry ingredients. Stir into the eggs and chocolate. Mix well, cover and refrigerate

FOR THE CHOCOLATE GANACHE
Heat the cream. Stir in and melt chocolate. Transfer to a small bowl and refrigerate until hard.

TO ASSEMBLE
Brush the inside of four 4 ounce soufflé cups with melted butter. Using an ice cream scoop, portion the cake batter between the soufflé cups.

Using a smaller scoop, portion the chocolate ganache in the center of the soufflé cups.

Place the cups on a baking sheet and into a 350 degree oven for 20 minutes or until the cakes have risen and are fairly firm. Serve at once with fresh berries, sweetened cream or both.

6 Course Chef's Summer Tasting Menu

First Course
Chilled Melon and Basil Soup with Chantilly Cream
Wine Pairing: 2010 Château de Pampelonne, Côtes de Provence Rosé, France

Second Course
Eggplant and Summer Tomato Tartlet

Third Course
Digby Bay Scallops Wrapped in Cedar with Gremolata Beurre Blanc
Wine Pairing: 2006 Ramey Chardonnay Hyde Vineyard, Carneros

Fourth Course
Wild Mushroom Soufflé with Shaved Gruyère and Velouté
Wine Pairing: 2007 Gundlach Bundschu Mountain Cuvee, Sonoma

Fifth Course
Petite Chateaubriand
Wine Pairing: 2001 Château Piganeau-Saint Emilion Grand Cru, France

Sixth Course
Crêpes with Peaches and Champagne

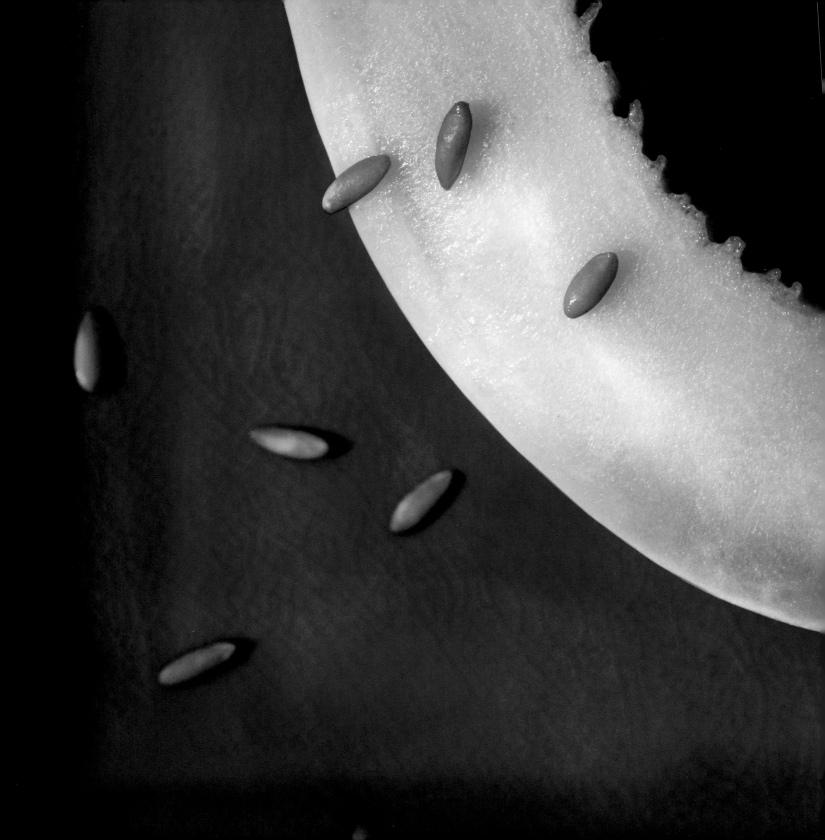

CHILLED MELON AND BASIL SOUP WITH CHANTILLY CREAM

[serves 4]

1 cup honeydew melon, peeled and seeded
1 pint apple juice, all natural/no sugar
½ cup heavy whipping cream
¼ cup sour cream
3 tbsp. honey
½ vanilla bean, seeded
3 tbsp. powdered sugar
4 ounces basil, chopped fine
sea salt to taste

It is important to pick a ripe melon. After the melon has been peeled and seeded, dice it small. Purée the melon in a food processor. Remove to a large bowl. Add apple juice. Mix well and add sour cream, stirring until incorporated. Add honey and basil and season to taste with sea salt. Refrigerate at least one hour before serving.

In a stainless steel bowl, combine powdered sugar, vanilla bean seeds and cream. Vigorously whisk until softly whipped. Serve as an accompaniment to the soup.

EGGPLANT AND SUMMER TOMATO TARTLET

[serves 4]

1 small eggplant, peeled and diced large
2 tbsp. fresh oregano leaves roughly chopped
¼ cup gouda cheese, shredded
2 shallots, peeled and julienned
4 sprigs oregano, leaves only
2 tomatoes, homegrown and diced
2 cloves garlic, thinly slivered

4 tbsp. olive oil, extra virgin
4 Cottage tart dough shells, 3"shells *(page 164)*
1 tsp. lemon juice, freshly squeezed
drizzle of lavender honey
sea salt and cracked black pepper as needed

In a sauté pan, heat 2 tablespoons of olive oil over medium-high setting. Add shallots and oregano and quickly sauté until vegetables are soft. Add eggplant and continue to sauté for 7 to 10 minutes or until soft. Add lemon juice and adjust the seasoning. Set aside and allow cooling.

In a second sauté pan, heat the remaining olive oil over medium-high setting. Add slivered garlic and sauté until soft. Add tomatoes and lavender honey. Reduce to a simmer for 7to 10 minutes. Taste for seasoning needs. Keep warm and set aside.

Fill the four tart shells evenly with the eggplant. Generously top with gouda. Place into a pre-heated 400 degree oven and bake until tart dough is a pale brown ten to fifteen minutes. Serve immediately with the warm tomato.

Digby Bay Scallops Wrapped in Cedar with Gremolata Beurre Blanc

[serves 4]

To Prepare the Scallops
8 fresh Digby Bay Canadian scallops
4 cedar papers, 3" x 5" sheets
½ cup chardonnay, dry
sea salt, course as needed

For the Gremolata Beurre Blanc
2 cloves garlic, crushed
½ tsp. lemon zest, finely grated
1 tsp. curly leaf parsley, chopped fine
1 tbsp. white wine vinegar
1 tbsp. chardonnay
⅛ cup cream
4 ounces butter, unsalted
salt and cracked pepper to taste

For Scallops
Soak cedar sheets in the chardonnay. Place two scallops on each sheet. Season the scallops with sea salt. Roll the cedar sheet, wrapping the scallops. Place wrapped scallops in a baking dish. Pour remaining wine in the dish.

Place the scallops into a 375 degree oven for 7 to 10 minutes or until the scallops are firm. To serve, place the cedar rolls on a serving platter. Unwrap and ladle the beurre blanc over the scallops.

For the Gremolata Beurre Blanc
Combine garlic, vinegar and wine in a sauce pot. Bring to a simmer over medium heat. Reduce the liquid to nearly full evaporation. Add cream and bring to a simmer. Reduce cream a touch and whisk in butter. Adjust seasoning with salt and pepper. Add parsley and lemon zest and serve.

WILD MUSHROOM SOUFFLÉ WITH SHAVED GRUYÈRE AND VELOUTÉ

[serves 4]

FOR SOUFFLÉ
4 egg whites
3 egg yolks
½ cup cream
1 shallot, minced
¼ lb. fresh chanterelles, washed
1 ounce clarified butter
1 tbsp. cornstarch
1 tbsp. water
1 tsp. lemon juice
1 tsp. sugar

salt and white pepper as needed
Gruyère cheese, wedge as needed
VELOUTÉ SAUCE
2 cups Cottage chicken stock *(page 167)*
2 ounce all-purpose flour
1 ounce clarified butter
salt and cracked white pepper as needed

Heat clarified butter in a sauce pan. Add shallots and gently sauté until onions are soft. Add chanterelles and sauté until soft. Add cream and heat to just a simmer. Allow cream to reduce by half.

Whisk together water and cornstarch in a separate dish. Add this to the simmering cream. Stirring frequently, cook cream until it is very thick or paste like. Adjust seasoning with salt and pepper. Refrigerate until cool. This is the soufflé base.

In a large, stainless steel bowl, whisk together the yolks and the cooled cream paste, mixing well. Set aside.

Using an upright kitchen mixer, whisk the egg whites and sugar on high. When the egg whites start to form soft peaks, add lemon juice. The lemon juice will help to stabilize the egg whites. Continue to mix until very stiff peaks form. Fold half of the egg whites into the yolk mixture. Gently fold until well mixed and add the remaining egg whites, mixing well again.

Prepare four 4 inch soufflé cups by brushing with butter and coating with finely ground bread crumbs. Portion the soufflé mixture evenly into the cups. Be sure that each soufflé has a generous amount of mushrooms. Fill them so that the peaks of the mixture stand above the soufflé cups. Your soufflé mix should be very stiff. Place into a 375 degree oven. Bake soufflés until golden brown and firm, between 15 and 20 minutes. Finish the soufflé by shaving Gruyère over the tops with a potato peeler.

FOR THE VELOUTÉ SAUCE
Mix the flour and butter and set aside. Bring chicken stock to a simmer. Whisk in flour and butter mixture. Stir frequently. Reduce heat to low and allow simmering for an additional five minutes. Adjust the seasoning with salt and pepper.

Petite Chateaubriand

[serves 4]

4 beef fillets, 4 ounce steak
2 cups beef stock
¼ cup white wine
1 tbsp. shallots, minced
2 cloves fresh garlic, minced
2 tbsp. fresh tarragon, finely chopped
drizzle of olive oil, extra virgin
1 ounce butter, melted
2 ounces all-purpose flour
sea salt and cracked black pepper as needed

Try 1 oz flour and still use 1 oz butter (2 tbsp) to see if flour dissolves better & sauce is thinner and browner)

Heat olive oil in a sauce pan over a high setting. Add the four steaks. Sear on both sides until brown. Remove to a baking tray lined with a roasting rack. Season steaks with salt and pepper. Place steaks in a pre-heated 375 degree oven for no more than 10 minutes, medium rare to medium temperature.

try 12 minutes

Meanwhile, add the shallots and garlic to pan and sauté until soft. Add white wine and reduce by half. Add beef stock and simmer for five minutes.

In a separate bowl, combine together the flour and melted butter. Mix well and add to the simmering sauce. Simmer until thickened. Add fresh tarragon and serve sauce over the fillet steaks.

Strain sauce if lumpy

CRÊPES WITH PEACHES AND CHAMPAGNE

[serves 4]

FOR PEACHES
2 Missouri peaches, cored and sliced
1 cup champagne
2 tbsp. peach brandy
¾ cup sugar
pinch of salt

FOR CRÊPES
1 cup all-purpose flour
2 tbsp. sugar
pinch of salt
2 eggs, cracked and whisked
¼ cup soda water
¾ cup milk, whole

FOR THE PEACHES
This part of the recipe should be prepared the day before.

Combine all ingredients and refrigerate at least 24 hours.

FOR CRÊPES
Combine all ingredients and mix well. Allow to chill for no less than thirty minutes.

Heat a ten inch, non-stick sauté pan. Spray the pan with food release (Pam®). Ladle four ounces of batter into the pan. Swirl pan to evenly distribute the batter. Cook crêpes until slightly brown. Turn the crêpes over gently with a rubber spatula and, again, cook until browned.

Serve the crêpes folded and topped with the macerated peaches. Garnish with whipped cream if desired.

6 Course Chef's Summer Tasting Menu

First Course
White Corn Bisque with Bacon and Gruyère Croquette
Wine Pairing: 2009 Shaya Verdejo Old Vine, Spain

Second Course
Caprese Salad
Dressed with Extra Virgin Olive Oil and Sea Salt

Third Course
Hickory Smoked Prawns with Tomato Coulis
Wine Pairing: 2009 Terredora di Paolo Falanghina Irpinia, Italy

Fourth Course
Potato Dauphinois with Chive Blossom and Shaved Truffles
Wine Pairing: 2005 Ponzi Pinot Noir, Willamette Valley Reserve, Oregon

Fifth Course
Coq au Vin
Wine Pairing: 2000 Château Yon-Figeac-Emilion Grand Cru, France

Sixth Course
Sabayon with Fresh Summer Berries and Grilled Pound Cake

White Corn Bisque with Bacon and Gruyère Croquette

[serves 4]

1 ½ cups white corn, cobbed
½ sweet Vidalia onion, diced fine
1 clove garlic, peeled and crushed
1 tsp. amber or dark corn syrup
2 ounces butter, melted
3 ounces flour
1 quart Cottage chicken stock *(page 167)*
½ cup heavy cream
sea salt to taste
4 strips bacon, diced and rendered crispy
Cottage Gruyère croquette *(page 165)*

Add 1 ounce of butter to a soup pot and place over medium heat. Add onions, corn and garlic. Sauté until tender. Add chicken stock and corn syrup. Cover and simmer for 30 minutes.

Meanwhile, mix flour and remaining butter together. Whisk into simmering soup, stirring constantly. Cover and simmer for another three minutes. Stir in cream and adjust the seasoning with salt and pepper

Prepare the Cottage Gruyère croquette. Mix in the crispy rendered bacon and cook according to instructions. Serve the croquettes on the side with the white corn bisque.

Caprese Salad Dressed with Extra Virgin Olive Oil and Sea Salt

[serves 4]

> 16 slices fresh tomatoes
> 16 fresh basil leaves
> 16 slices fresh mozzarella
> 1 tbsp. fine balsamic vinegar, 20 year + aged
> 2 tbsp. fine olive oil, extra virgin
> sprinkle of sea salt, course grind

This recipe requires the best of the best. Homegrown tomatoes and fresh basil are needed. For plating, alternately stack the tomatoes, basil and mozzarella. Drizzle each plate with olive oil and balsamic. Sprinkle with sea salt and enjoy.

Hickory Smoked Prawns with Tomato Coulis

[serves 4]

8 fresh gulf coast jumbo shrimp, peeled and deveined
1 tbsp. olive oil, extra virgin
2 cups hickory chips, soaked in water
3 cloves fresh garlic, slivered
¼ white onion, diced fine
2 tomatoes, peeled and seeded
¼ cup Cottage chicken stock *(page 167)*
crushed red pepper to taste
drizzle of honey
sea salt, course, as needed

Pour a tablespoon of olive oil into a sauce pot. Heat the olive oil on a high setting and add shrimp. Brown the shrimp on both sides and set to the side. The shrimp will not be fully cooked at this time.

Add garlic, crushed red pepper and white onions to the pan and return to medium heat. Sauté vegetables until translucent. Add chicken stock. Be sure to scrape the bottom of the pan to release the shrimp 'fond'.

Dice tomatoes fine and add to sauce pan. Stir well and bring to a simmer. Add honey and adjust the seasoning with the sea salt. Turn stove setting to low.

Wrap the soaked wood chips in aluminum foil. Use a fork to poke holes through the foil. Place the foiled wood chips on an outdoor grill set to high. Allow for a good smoke to develop. Place shrimp on the grill. Close the lid and cook 3 to 5 minutes or until firm and white. Adjust the seasoning with salt and pepper.

Serve the shrimp immediately with the tomato coulis and, if you like, fresh lemon.

Potato Dauphinois with Chive Blossom and Shaved Truffles

[serves 4]

16 assorted baby potatoes, washed
⅓ cup Gruyère cheese, shredded
2 cups cream
¼ cup sauvignon blanc
½ shallot, minced
2 cloves fresh garlic, slivered thin
1 tsp. fresh thyme leaves, chopped fine
1 ounce clarified butter
salt and cracked white pepper as needed
2 tbsp. black truffle peelings
4 fresh chive blossoms

Begin by boiling the baby potatoes in salted water. Cook potatoes until al dente. Drain and set aside.

In a sauce pot, heat clarified butter over medium heat. Add shallots, garlic and thyme leaves. Sauté vegetables until translucent in appearance. Add wine and cream. Adjust seasoning with salt and pepper. Do not over season; the cream will reduce when baked, therefore concentrating flavors. Bring the cream to a simmer and remove from heat.

Halve the length of the potatoes with a paring knife and place them in a baking dish. Pour cream over the potatoes and cover with foil. Place dish in a 375 degree oven and bake for thirty minutes or until the cream has smoothly thickened. Remove foil and cover the potatoes with Gruyère. Turn the oven setting to 'broil'. Brown the cheese and serve with truffle peelings. Garnish with fresh chive blossoms.

Coq au Vin

[serves 4]

4 fresh chicken thighs, skin on
1 cup white button mushrooms, quartered
½ yellow onion, diced large
1 carrot, peeled and sliced
½ stalk celery, peeled and diced large
3 cloves garlic, slivered
1 tbsp. fresh thyme leaves, chopped fine

1 pint Cottage chicken stock *(page 167)*
1 pint burgundy wine
6 strips bacon, diced large
1 ounce clarified butter
2 bay leaves
salt and cracked black pepper as needed
2 ounces all purpose flour

Start by marinating chicken with one cup of the red wine and fresh thyme. Refrigerate 2 to 4 hours before continuing.

Heat clarified butter in a large sauté pan. Add bacon and render until crispy. Remove the bacon and drain on a paper towel. Add chicken thighs to the sauté pan and return to medium heat. Brown the chicken on both sides and remove to a deep baking dish. Season the chicken with salt and pepper.

Add flour to the pan and mix well with the rendered oil. Add remaining red wine and chicken stock. Bring to a boil and adjust the seasoning. Pour the sauce over the chicken.

Place the remaining vegetables atop chicken. Mix all ingredients well, cover with foil and place in a 325 degree oven for one hour or until chicken is tender. Serve with the rendered bacon.

SABAYON WITH FRESH SUMMER BERRIES AND GRILLED POUND CAKE

[serves 4]

FOR THE SABAYON
5 egg yolks
¼ cup sugar
splash of chardonnay

FOR THE SUMMER BERRIES AND GRILLED POUND CAKE
¼ cup available fresh berries
3 tbsp. Grand Marnier
drizzle of lavender honey
4 slices of pound cake, 2 ounce slices
2 ounces clarified butter

FOR THE SABAYON
Combine sugar and yolks in a stainless steel bowl. Temper the mixture. Place over a heated water bath and whisk vigorously until mixture is pale yellow and thickened. Add wine and serve immediately.

FOR THE SUMMER BERRIES AND GRILLED POUND CAKE
Heat butter in a sauté pan. When butter is crackling, place cake slices in pan. Grill pound cake on each side until golden brown. Serve immediately with the sabayon and fresh berries.

AUTUMN

6 Course Chef's Autumn Tasting Menu

First Course
Roasted Butternut Squash Soup with Maple and Brie Cheese Croquette
Wine Pairing: 2009 Willakenzie Pinot Blanc, Willamette Valley, Oregon

Second Course
Seared Foie Gras with Cranberry Compote, Black Sesame Tuile and Autumn Greens

Third Course
Sautéed Skate Wing with Lemon and Capers
Wine Pairing: 2008 Lafite Val de L'Ours Chardonnay, France

Fourth Course
Fried Sage and Sweet Potato Tartlet
Wine Pairing: 2007 Châteauneuf-du-Pape Bosquet des Papes, France

Fifth Course
Smoked Beef Short Ribs with Anise Au Jus
Wine Pairing: 2007 Silverado Cabernet Sauvignon, California

Sixth Course
Petite Apple Tarte Tatin
Wine Pairing: 2006 Château de Cosse, Sauternes, France

ROASTED BUTTERNUT SQUASH SOUP WITH MAPLE AND BRIE CHEESE CROQUETTE

[serves 4]

1 small butternut squash, peeled and diced medium
½ cup cream, heavy whipping
1 ½ quarts Cottage chicken stock *(page 167)*
2 tbsp. yellow onion, fine diced
1 tbsp. butter, unsalted
¼ cup white wine, dry
2 tbsp. honey

nutmeg, fresh grated to taste
1 bay leaf
2 ounces butter, melted
3 ounces all-purpose flour
sea salt and cracked pepper to taste
maple and brie croquettes *(page 165)*
2 tbsp. Vermont Grade A maple syrup
3 ounces melted brie cheese

Combine half of the melted butter and butternut squash in a stainless steel bowl. Season with grated nutmeg, salt and pepper. Transfer to a baking sheet, cover with foil and place in a pre-heated 375 degree oven. Roast the squash for 20 to 30 minutes or until tender. Set aside.

Heat remaining butter in a soup pot over medium heat. Add onions and gently sauté for a couple of minutes or until the vegetables are tender. Add remaining ingredients, including the reserved butternut squash but excluding the cream, melted butter and flour. Cover and simmer for 30 minutes.

Combine flour and butter. Whisk into the simmering soup. Stir constantly as the soup thickens.

When ready, finish the soup with cream and serve immediately with the maple and brie croquettes on the side.

For the croquettes, use the Cottage Gruyère croquette recipe. To this, add 2 tablespoons of Vermont Grade A maple syrup and substitute 3 ounces of melted brie cheese for the Gruyère. Combine well and proceed with remaining cooking instructions.

SEARED FOIE GRAS WITH CRANBERRY COMPOTE, BLACK SESAME TUILE AND AUTUMN GREENS

[serves 4]

4 fresh foie gras, sliced to 4 ounces
8 leaves of locally grown butter lettuce, washed

FOR THE CRANBERRY COMPOTE
1 cup fresh cranberries, whole
1 ¼ cup red wine, pinot noir
½ cup water
1 tbsp. white vinegar
¾ cup sugar
pinch dried orange peel
sea salt as needed
2 tbsp. butter, unsalted

FOR THE TUILE
½ cup all-purpose flour
½ cup sugar, confectioner's
pinch sea salt
5 ounces egg whites (approximately 3 eggs)
2 ½ tsp. melted butter, unsalted
1 tbsp. whole milk
1 tbsp. black sesame seeds

In a sauce pot, combine cranberries, wine, water, sugar and orange peel. Simmer gently until the liquid coats the back of a spoon. Add butter and sea salt.

Sift together flour, sugar and sea salt. In a separate bowl, lightly whisk the egg whites until opaque and foamy. Add egg whites to sifted flour mixture. Mix until incorporated. Add butter and milk. Mix well and set aside. Allow batter to chill for one hour.

Line a baking tray with a non-stick baking mat. Spoon batter onto the baking mat. Spread batter evenly and thinly into 4" circles. Sprinkle batter with sesame seeds. Repeat this three more times. Place cookies into a preheated 350 degree oven for 7 to 10 minutes or until golden brown. Remove and very gently place on a cooling rack.

Arrange the lettuce leaves, 2 each per person, on a chilled plate. Keep cool.

Heat a sauté pan at high temperature until searing hot. Add the slices of liver to the pan. Sprinkle with salt. Sear each side for no more than two minutes. Serve immediately over the arranged lettuce leaves. Dress the dish with the cranberry compote and top with black sesame tuile.

SAUTÉED SKATE WING WITH LEMON AND CAPERS

[serves 4]

4 fresh skate wings, 5 ounce portions
2 cups fish stock
fresh lemon juice from 1 lemon
¼ cup capers
1 shallot, julienned
3 cloves garlic, slivered
2 scallions, slivered
¼ cup corn meal
¼ cup rice flour

sea salt as needed
¼ cup olive oil
1 ounce butter, melted
2 ounces all-purpose flour

In a sauce pot, heat two tablespoons olive oil. Add shallots and garlic. Gently sauté for 3 to 4 minutes or until the onions and garlic are soft. Add fish stock and rise to a simmer. Add lemon juice and capers. Simmer for 5 minutes.

Combine butter and all-purpose flour in a separate container. Mix well and add to simmering stock. Reduce heat to low and allow to cook for an additional 5 minutes. Adjust the seasoning and add the scallions just prior serving with the fish.

Meanwhile, heat a skillet over high and add remaining olive oil. Sift together rice flour and corn meal. Dust the skate wing in the flour mixture and place in pan. Pan fry until golden brown and crispy. Serve at once with caper, lemon and scallion sauce.

FRIED SAGE AND SWEET POTATO TARTLET

[serves 4]

    2 sweet potatoes, peeled and quartered
    1 tbsp. Vidalia onion, minced
    2 ounces Brie cheese, rind off
    1 tbsp. lavender honey
    1 egg, cracked and beaten
    sea salt as needed
    pinch of white pepper, ground
    8 fresh sage leaves
    olive oil as needed
    4 -2 ounces Cottage tart dough *(page 164)*

Boil sweet potatoes in salted water for 20 to 30 minutes or until very soft. Drain in a colander and let stand 5 minutes; the potatoes must be well drained. Transfer to a stainless steel bowl and fold in Brie cheese. The cheese will evenly melt. Fold in whisked egg and mash the mixture. Add white pepper, honey and season to your liking with sea salt. Wrap and chill for 20 minutes.

Heat a small sauté pan and drizzle a couple of tablespoons of olive oil in the pan. Heat the oil at a medium setting and add the shallots. Sauté until soft and translucent. Take care not to burn or even toast them. Add the onions to the sweet potato mixture and mix well.

Roll out chilled tart dough to a thin circle. Line a non-stick, 4 inch tart pan with the dough. Firmly form dough to the pan. Repeat process.

Fill tart shells with the sweet potato mixture. Level the filling and place into a 350 degree oven. Bake for 30 to 40 minutes, rotating once, or until the filling is firm and the tart golden.

Meanwhile, heat a quarter cup of olive oil in a sauté pan to around 400 degrees. Place sage leaves into the hot oil. Please be careful, as the water content of the sage will mix with the hot oil and splatter. Fry the sage to a deep green and remove to a plate lined with a paper towel. Sprinkle sage with sea salt and serve with the freshly baked sweet potato tart.

SMOKED BEEF SHORT RIBS WITH ANISE AU JUS

[serves 4]

1 ½ pounds choice beef short ribs, trimmed/bone in
1 cup hickory wood chips, soaked in water
2 cups beef stock
8 ounces butter, unsalted
1 tbsp. shallots, minced
1 stalk celery, peeled and minced
¼ cup red wine, cabernet sauvignon
1 ounce clarified butter
2 ounces all-purpose flour

2 bay leaves
sea salt and cracked pepper as needed
¼ tsp. anise oil
1 cheesecloth

Heat a medium sized sauté pan on high heat. Add a drizzle of clarified butter. Sear each side of the beef ribs until brown. Transfer beef to a roasting pan and just cover with water. Season water generously with salt and cracked pepper. Add bay leaves and half pound of whole butter. Cover with foil and braise in a 325 degree oven for 1 ½ hours or until fork tender but not falling off of the bone.

Meanwhile, add wine to the sauté pan and, over medium to high heat, work the fond or, the meat bits stuck to the pan, off with a whisk or kitchen spoon. Add beef stock and bring to a simmer. Strain liquid through cheesecloth and set aside.

Heat a sauté pan over medium heat. Drizzle a bit of clarified butter in the pan and add onions and celery. Cook until soft. Add strained stock and bring to a simmer. Mix anise oil, clarified butter and flour together. The roux should have a paste-like consistency. Add the roux to the simmering stock. Whisk thoroughly and reduce until sauce coats the back of a spoon. Adjust the seasoning and keep warm.

Carefully place the ribs on a non-stick roasting rack and set aside.

Adjust the setting on your outdoor grill to high. Wrap the soaked wood chips in aluminum foil. Poke holes in the foil wrapper and place onto the grill. Close the top. When the chips are producing steady smoke, place the beef ribs on the grill. Cook for no more than 15 minutes. Season with sea salt and serve with au jus.

Petite Apple Tarte Tatin

[serves 4]

    4 Gala apples, peeled and cored
    1 cup brown sugar
    4 ounces butter, unsalted and melted
    pinch of sea salt
    1 sheet puff pastry
    dusting of all-purpose flour

Thinly and evenly slice apples and set aside. Combine brown sugar, butter and salt in a sauce pan. Bring the mixture to a simmer stirring frequently. Simmer until all sugar has melted. Remove from the heat and set aside to cool.

Evenly divide the mixture between four 4 in. non-stick tart pans. Carefully arrange the apples in the pans. A circular pattern is desired but not necessary.

Dust a clean worktop counter with flour.   Roll out pastry to half the original thickness. Cut four squares evenly.

Place the pastry on top of the apples. Repeat this for the remaining three tarts. Sprinkle with sugar and place into a preheated 375 degree oven. Bake until puff pastry tops are a rich golden brown and the syrupy liquid is bubbling, approximately 30 minutes.

When tarts are ready, remove them from the oven and allow to cool slightly. Invert them by placing a plate over the tart and then carefully turning it over. Please be careful as the liquid will be hot.

Serve the tart alone or accompanied by whipped cream or vanilla ice cream.

6 Course Chef's Autumn Tasting Menu

First Course
Potato and Leek Soup with Pecans and Country Ham
Wine Pairing: 2008 Groth Sauvignon Blanc, Napa Valley

Second Course
Burgundy Poached Pear with Beet Micro-Greens and Blue Cheese Soufflé

Third Course
Roasted Monkfish Finished with Sherry
Wine Pairing: 2009 Piattelli Premium Torrontés, Argentina

Fourth Course
Pumpkin Risotto with Shaved Pecorino
Wine Pairing: 2004 Produttori del Barbaresco Rio Sordo Riserva, Italy

Fifth Course
Roulade of Beef with Fresh Sorrel and Gruyère
Wine Pairing: 2006 Clos de l'Oratoire Châteauneuf-du-Pape, France

Sixth Course
Persimmon Sorbet

Potato and Leek Soup with Pecans and Country Ham

[serves 4]

2 russet potatoes, peeled and diced
1 cup leeks, washed and diced
1 ½ quarts Cottage chicken stock *(page 167)*
½ cup chablis
3 cloves garlic, crushed
1 tbsp. shallot, minced
2 ounces butter, softened
½ cup heavy cream
3 ounces pecans, toasted and chopped
4 ounces smoked country ham, diced
sea salt and cracked pepper to taste

Heat a teaspoon of softened butter in a soup pot. Reserve the remaining butter for later use.

Add garlic and shallots to soup pot and sauté for a minute or two or until the vegetables appear translucent. Add the chablis, chicken stock, leeks, potatoes and ham. Cover and simmer for 30 to 45 minutes. Add cream and butter, stirring frequently. Season to taste and serve immediately with chopped and toasted pecans.

BURGUNDY POACHED PEAR WITH BEET MICRO-GREENS AND BLUE CHEESE SOUFFLÉ

[serves 4]

FOR THE POACHED PEAR
2 Anjou pears
1 cinnamon stick
1 quart red table wine
1 ½ cups sugar
1 tsp. dried orange peel
3 cloves
pinch of sea salt, course
1 cup beet micro-greens, for garnish

FOR THE SOUFFLÉ
4 egg whites
3 egg yolks
½ cup cream
2 ounces Maytag blue cheese
1 shallot, minced
1 ounce clarified butter
1 tbsp. cornstarch
1 tbsp. water
1 tsp. lemon juice
1 tsp. sugar
salt and white pepper as needed

Peel the pears and put in a sauce pot. Add all remaining ingredients and place on a stove setting of low. Bring to a very slow simmer for 10 minutes or until the pears are soft and rich in color. Allow pears to cool with the poaching liquid. Refrigerate until needed.

Heat clarified butter in a sauce pan. Add shallots and gently sauté until the onions are soft. Add cream and heat to just a simmer. Whisk together water and cornstarch in a separate dish. Add this to the cream. Stir cream until it is very thick or paste like. Crumble the blue cheese into the cream. Fold until all of the cheese is evenly melted. Adjust the seasoning with salt and pepper. Refrigerate until cool.

In a large stainless steel bowl, whisk together the yolks and the cooled cream sauce, mixing well. Set aside.

Using an upright kitchen mixer, whisk egg whites and sugar on high. When egg whites start to form soft peaks, add lemon juice. The lemon juice will help to stabilize the egg whites. Continue to mix until very stiff peaks. Fold half of the egg whites into yolk mixture. Gently fold until well mixed and add the remaining egg whites, mixing well again.

Prepare four 4 in. soufflé cups by brushing with butter and coating with finely ground bread crumbs. Portion the soufflé mixture evenly into cups. Fill so that the peaks of the mixture stand above the soufflé cups; your soufflé mix should be very stiff. Place into a 375 degree oven. Bake soufflés until golden brown and firm, between 15 and 20 minutes.

Meanwhile, cut pears in half and, with a melon baller, take the core out and discard. Evenly slice pears and place them on a plate atop washed fresh beet micro-greens. Place freshly baked soufflé on the plate and drizzle a bit of the poaching liquid onto ingredients. Serve immediately.

Roasted Monkfish Finished with Sherry

[serves 4]

> 4 monkfish tails, trimmed, 4 ounce portions
> 2 shallots, peeled and quartered
> 3 cloves garlic, peeled and smashed
> 4 sprigs thyme
> 2 ounces clarified butter
> 2 tbsp. pecans, toasted and crushed
> ¼ cup sherry, dry
> ¼ cup cream
> salt and pepper to taste

Heat clarified butter in a large oven-proof sauté pan on a high setting. Add monkfish pieces, shallots, and garlic. Brown the fish and place into a preheated 400 degree oven for 7 to 10 minutes, turning fish and vegetables frequently.

When fish is cooked, remove the pieces from pan and add sherry. Place back on the stove top at a medium setting and allow sherry to reduce by half. Add cream, thyme and pecans. Reduce until cream thickens slightly. Season with salt and pepper. Serve by pouring the sauce over the fish.

Pumpkin Risotto with Shaved Pecorino

[serves 4]

    1 fresh small pie pumpkin, diced medium
    2 cloves garlic, peeled and slivered
    1 tbsp. shallots, minced
    1 quart Cottage chicken stock, hot *(page 167)*
    ½ cup arborio rice
    3 tbsp. clarified butter
    3 tbsp. cream
    pinch of nutmeg
    sea salt and cracked pepper to taste

Heat clarified butter in a sauce pot. Add shallots, garlic and pumpkin. Sauté gently until onions and garlic are soft. Add rice and continue to sauté, stirring frequently, for an additional minute or two.

Add one cup of chicken stock. Frequently stir with a wooden spoon until stock has been absorbed. Add additional stock and continue this process until rice is cooked, about 20 minutes.

When the rice is fully cooked, add the cream and nutmeg. Season with sea salt and cracked black pepper.

ROULADE OF BEEF WITH FRESH SORREL AND GRUYÈRE

[serves 4]

4 beef fillets, 3 ounce medallion
1 cup Gruyère, shredded
4 fresh sorrel, leaves large
¼ cup bread crumbs, fine
2 eggs, cracked and whisked
¼ cup flour for dusting
1 pint canola oil for frying
2 cups beef stock
¼ cup white wine
1 tbsp. shallots, minced
2 cloves fresh garlic, minced

drizzle of olive oil, extra virgin
2 tbsp. butter, melted
3 tbsp. all-purpose flour
sea salt and cracked black pepper as needed

Flatten out each medallion to about ¹⁄₁₆ inch with a mallet. Lay each medallion on a clean and flat surface.   Season each slice with salt and pepper. Layer with one leaf of sorrel and then the Gruyère cheese. Once complete, roll each slice. Trim the edges with a knife for presentation purposes.

Dust each roll with flour. Dip in the whisked egg and then cover with bread crumbs.

In a sauce pot, heat the canola oil to 400 degrees. Carefully dip each beef roll in the hot oil and pan-fry until golden brown. Remove and allow to rest on a clean kitchen towel.

Meanwhile, heat olive oil in a sauce pan over a high setting. Add shallots and garlic to the pan and sauté until soft. Add white wine and reduce by half. Add beef stock and simmer for five minutes.

In a separate bowl, combine together the flour and melted butter. Mix well and add to the simmering sauce. Simmer until thickened. Serve over the roulade.

Persimmon Sorbet

[serves 4]

    2 persimmons, very ripe
    1 ⅛ cup sugar
    3 tbsp. lemon juice, fresh
    3 tbsp. sparkling water
    drizzle of Grand Marnier
    1 tsp. fresh mint, finely chopped

Make sure the persimmons are very ripe. Peel the fruit, and cut the flesh into cubes. Add all ingredients to a food processor and puree until sugar is dissolved.

Using an electric ice cream/sorbet maker, add the puree to a frozen ice cream maker bowl. Churn the mixture according to the manufacturer's instruction. When frozen, place into a freezer overnight. Serve with a drizzle of Grand Marnier and fresh mint.

6 Course Chef's Autumn Tasting Menu

First Course
Consommé Brunoise
Wine Pairing: Emilio Lustau Puerto Fino, Solera Reserva, Spain

Second Course
Tart Missouri Apples with Goat Cheese and Breakfast Radish
Finished with Cider Vinaigrette

Third Course
Oven Roasted Pike with Cabbage and Smoked Bacon
Wine Pairing: 2008 Chalk Hill Sauvignon Blanc, Russian River Valley

Fourth Course
Root Vegetable Gratin
Wine Pairing: 2009 Féraud, Brunel Côtes du Rhône, France

Fifth Course
Osso Bucco á la Provençale
Wine Pairing: 2007 Luce La Vite Lucente Toscana, Italy

Sixth Course
Candied Pumpkin Tartlet

CONSOMMÉ BRUNOISE

[serves 4]

    1 quart Cottage chicken stock *(page 167)*
    1 pound ground chicken (or turkey)
    5 ounces egg whites, whisked lightly
    1 carrot, peeled and diced fine
    ¼ cup leeks, washed and diced fine
    1 stalk celery, peeled and diced fine
    1 tbsp. fresh tarragon, chopped fine
    cheesecloth

In a soup pot, bring chicken stock to a simmer. In another stainless steel bowl, combine egg whites and ground chicken and mix together well. Stir this mixture into the simmering chicken stock. Cover and simmer on low for 30 minutes. Strain the chicken stock through a sieve and cheesecloth. Return to the stovetop, heat and bring to a simmer. Add carrots, leek, and celery. Season with salt and pepper. Simmer for a couple of minutes and serve immediately with a generous sprinkle of tarragon.

Tart Missouri Apples with Goat Cheese and Breakfast Radish

[serves 4]

    2 Missouri apples, peeled and diced large
    8 French breakfast radishes, washed
    3 ounces goat cheese, crumbled
    handful of baby arugula, washed
    2 tbsp. apple cider
    1 tsp. apple cider vinegar
    1 tsp. olive oil, light
    1 tbsp. honey
    sea salt and white pepper as needed

Boil radishes in salted water until tender. Strain and soak in ice water. Cut radishes in half and place into a salad bowl. Add apples, goat cheese and arugula. Cover and refrigerate.

In a stainless steel bowl, whisk together cider, vinegar, olive oil and honey. Adjust the seasoning with salt and pepper.

Dress the greens with vinaigrette. Serve on a tray or individually.

Oven Roasted Pike with Cabbage and Smoked Bacon

[serves 4]

    4 fresh Michigan pike fillets, skinned and boned, 5 ounces each
    5 ounces lardon or high quality bacon, diced large
    ¼ head white cabbage, diced large and cored
    ¼ yellow onion, diced large
    2 tbsp. plus 1 tsp. rice wine vinegar
    3 tbsp. lemon juice
    2 cloves fresh garlic, minced
    2 tbsp. plus 1 tsp. butter, whole and unsalted
    2 cloves, whole
    splash of chardonnay
    sea salt and cracked pepper as needed
    dusting of flour

Render bacon in a large cast iron pan over high heat until crisp around the edges. Remove bacon, leaving rendered oil in pan. Drain bacon and set aside.

Dust fish fillets entirely with flour. Then, shake fillets of any excess flour and place them in the hot bacon grease. Pan sear until fish is crispy and brown on all sides. Place on a baking tray lined with parchment paper and into a 350 degree oven for 10 minutes or until fish is flaky. Season fish after cooking.

While fish is cooking, add onions, cabbage and cloves to skillet. Sauté on high until vegetables are soft. Add wine and 1 teaspoon of rice wine vinegar and simmer. Adjust seasoning with salt and pepper. Add a teaspoon of butter, mix well and arrange on a serving platter.

Add lemon juice, garlic and remaining vinegar to skillet and return to high heat. Reduce mixture to almost dry, leaving no more than a teaspoon of liquid in the pan. Add butter, mix well and remove from heat

Arrange fish fillets on top of cabbage. Pour lemon butter over the fish and cabbage. Sprinkle dish with bacon. Serve at once.

ROOT VEGETABLE GRATIN

[serves 4]

    2 small baby gold potatoes, halved
    1 small sweet potato, peeled and sliced
    1 turnip, peeled and thinly sliced
    1 shallot, thinly sliced
    3 cloves garlic, minced
    1 ½ cups cream
    1 egg yolk, whisked
    splash of chablis
    ½ tsp. lemon juice
    3 ounces Gruyère cheese, shredded

In a sauce pot, heat lemon juice, chablis, garlic and shallots to a simmer. Allow liquid to reduce by half and then add cream. Slowly heat to a gentle simmer. Whisk egg yolk separately with some of the hot cream. Add the egg and cream mixture back to the cream. Simmer until cream is slightly thickened. Add Gruyère cheese and stir well to ensure even melting. Adjust the seasoning with salt and pepper.

Butter and then dust a 5 ½ in. soufflé cup with fine bread crumbs. Arrange various sliced vegetables in alternating order. Ladle sauce over to top, reserving some for plating. Cover gratin with foil and place into a 375 degree oven. Bake for thirty minutes or until vegetables are tender by the poke of a knife. If desired, brown the tops of the gratin by removing the foil and turning on your broiler briefly.

Cut the gratin to four portions. Spoon to four plates and finish with a drizzle of cream sauce. Serve with a sprinkling of fresh oregano leaves.

Osso Bucco á la Provençale

[serves 4]

4 veal shanks, 4" x 2" bone-in
4 cloves garlic, slivered
2 ounces pancetta ham, diced
2 tbsp. olive oil
1 yellow onion, diced
1 dozen calamata olives, pitted
1pint tomatoes, peeled, seeded and diced
1 cup red table wine
1 quart beef stock
1 tsp. tomato paste
1 tbsp. whole butter, unsalted

1 tbsp. fresh thyme leaves, chopped
1 tbsp. fresh oregano leaves, chopped
1 tbsp. water
1 tbsp. cornstarch
sea salt and cracked black pepper to taste
¼ tsp. dried orange peel

Render crispy the pancetta ham in a large sauce pan. Remove pancetta pieces to a paper towel and set aside.

Sear the veal shanks in pan. Take care that the meat is browned on both sides. Add garlic and onions and cook until soft. Add red wine, beef stock, olives, tomatoes and orange peel. Cover sauce pot with aluminum foil and place into a pre-heated 350 degree oven. Braise meat for no less than 2 hours or until fork tender.

Carefully place veal shanks on a large platter, keeping shanks intact with the bone.

Return the braising liquid to a medium heat and bring to a simmer. In a clean bowl, dissolve corn starch with 1 tbsp. water. Add cornstarch and water to the simmering sauce. Allow to thicken.

Add butter and chopped herbs. Ladle sauce over the veal. Sprinkle the crispy pancetta over the dish and serve.

CANDIED PUMPKIN TARTLET

[serves 4]

    4 Cottage tart dough shells, pre-baked 5" *(page 164)*
    ½ cup pumpkin, fresh mashed
    ½ cup cream, hot
    2 eggs, cracked
    ⅓ cup plus 2 tbsp. sugar
    pinch of sea salt
    pinch of cinnamon, ground

In a bowl, combine eggs and sugar. Mix well and add a touch of hot cream, whisking vigorously. Add the rest of the hot cream, pumpkin, cinnamon and salt. Mix well again and fill each tartlet shell three quarters full. Place the shells on a baking sheet lined with parchment paper and place into a 325 degree oven for 15 minutes or until the custard has set. Remove from oven and refrigerate at least 2 hours.

Sprinkle 2 tablespoons of sugar on top of the chilled tarts. With a blow torch or crème brulee torch, flame the sugared tops of the tarts until lightly browned. Serve with whipped cream and mint.

BASIC RECIPES

Cottage Tart Dough

[yields 8 tart shells, 3-5 in. each]

  2 ½ cups all-purpose flour
  1 tsp. sugar
  8 ounces butter, unsalted and chilled
  ⅓ cup ice water

In a food processor bowl, combine flour, salt and sugar. Add butter, and process until the mixture resembles coarse bread crumbs, about 8 to 10 seconds.

With machine running, add ice water in a slow stream through feed tube. Pulse the mixture until the dough holds together without being wet or sticky; be careful not to process more than 30 seconds. To test, squeeze a small amount together. If it is crumbly, add more ice water 1 tablespoon at a time.

Divide dough into two equal balls. Flatten each ball into a disc and wrap in plastic. Transfer to the refrigerator and chill at least 1 hour.

Remove dough from refrigerator. Roll out dough to 1/16 in. and form into 3-5 in. mini-tart shell moulds.

Cottage Gruyère Croquette

[yields 8 croquettes]

    1 cup flour
    2 eggs, cracked and whisked
    ¼ cup whole milk
    ½ cup Gruyère, shredded
    pinch of sea salt
    1 tbsp. baking powder
    1 cup bread crumbs
    1 quart oil for frying

Combine flour and sea salt in a bowl. In a separate bowl, whisk together eggs and milk. Add eggs and milk to the flour. Mix until well incorporated. Do not over mix. Fold in Gruyère cheese. Cover and refrigerate at least 30 minutes.

Heat oil to 400 degrees. Place bread crumbs in a shallow dish. Using a ½ ounce disher, scoop the croquette batter into the bread crumbs. Coat the croquette with bread crumbs and drop into hot oil. Fry until golden brown and cooked through. Serve immediately as a side accompaniment.

COTTAGE CHICKEN STOCK

[yields 2 quarts of stock]

    4 chicken thighs, skinless/bone-in
    ½ gallon water
    ½ cup leeks, washed and coarsely chopped
    1 carrot, coarsely chopped
    1 tomato, quartered
    1 stalk celery, coarsely chopped
    3 cloves garlic, crushed
    1 cube chicken bouillon
    1 tsp. turmeric
    1 clove, whole
    3 large sprigs tarragon, fresh
    3 tbsp. sea salt

Combine all ingredients in a stock pot and bring to a simmer over medium heat. Cover and cook for 1 hour. Strain and refrigerate.

SOURCES

FOOD SOURCES

Seasonal, Fresh Produce
Wiese Nursery and Produce
(636) 978-3213
www.wiesenursery.com

Truffles, Gourmet Specialty Items and Finishing Oils
Eurogourmet
(636) 970-6400

Seafood
Bob's Seafood
(314) 993-4844

MISC. SOURCES
Boys and Girls Clubs of St. Charles County
(636) 946-6255
www.bgc-stc.org

Carmen Troesser Photography
www.carmentroesser.com

Steven Cranford - Pixilated Pictures
(314) 766-7494
pixilatedpics@cs.com

RECIPE INDEX

NOTES